GET A LIFE

GET A LIFE

A Roadmap
to Rule the World

BOB FISCH

WITH BRUCE APAR

Forbes | Books

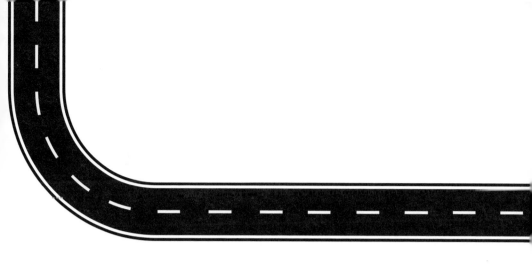

GET IN TOUCH WITH BOB!

FISCHTALES1

MILLENNIALBABYBOOMER.COM

BOB FISCH

BOB FISCH, MBB

FISCHTALES1

FISCHTALES

Published by ForbesBooks, Charleston, South Carolina.
Member of Advantage Media Group.

ForbesBooks is a registered trademark, and the ForbesBooks colophon is a trademark of Forbes Media, LLC.

Printed in the United States of America.

10 9 8 7 6 5 4 3 2 1

ISBN: 978-1-95588-450-1 (Hardcover)
ISBN: 978-1-95588-467-9 (eBook)

LCCN: 2022915020

Cover design by David Taylor.
Layout design by Wesley Strickland.

This custom publication is intended to provide accurate information and the opinions of the author in regard to the subject matter covered. It is sold with the understanding that the publisher, Forbes Books, is not engaged in rendering legal, financial, or professional services of any kind. If legal advice or other expert assistance is required, the reader is advised to seek the services of a competent professional.

Since 1917, Forbes has remained steadfast in its mission to serve as the defining voice of entrepreneurial capitalism. Forbes Books, launched in 2016 through a partnership with Advantage Media, furthers that aim by helping business and thought leaders bring their stories, passion, and knowledge to the forefront in custom books. Opinions expressed by Forbes Books authors are their own. To be considered for publication, please visit **books.Forbes.com**.

I dedicate this book to the many people who have touched my life. They made me realize how important it is to "give back" to help people achieve their dreams and goals. This includes writing this book to help with their roadmaps to rule their world.

I am grateful for and fortunate to have all my friends, associates, and family who inspire me with continued strength and love.

The best is yet to come!

A ROAD MAP TO RULE THE WORLD

1 HELLO, THIS IS YOUR CAREER CALLING

2 IT'S ALL IN THE TIMING

3 GET A VISION

4 GET CONFIDENT

9 TRIBAL KNOWLEDGE IS POWER

10 FEAR OF SUCCESS

11 WHATEVER IT TAKES

12 THE NEW ROARING '20s

CONTENTS

INTRODUCTION 1
THIS BOOK IS NOT FOR THE TIMID

CHAPTER 1 11
HELLO, THIS IS YOUR CAREER CALLING

CHAPTER 2 25
IT'S ALL IN THE TIMING

CHAPTER 3 35
**I TEACH THEM BUSINESS,
THEY TEACH ME LIFE!**

CHAPTER 4 53
GET A VISION

CHAPTER 5 69
IT'S ALL ABOUT PECPL

CHAPTER 6 87
EVERYBODY NEEDS A BUDDY!

CHAPTER 7 99
ROADMAP TO THE REST OF YOUR LIFE

CHAPTER 8 113
LEAD, FOLLOW, OR GET OUT OF THE WAY!

CHAPTER 9 127
TRIBAL KNOWLEDGE IS POWER

CHAPTER 10 141
SUCCESS IS FOR THE BRAVE!

CHAPTER 11 155
BACK TO THE FUTURE (A.K.A. "THE FEEL")

CHAPTER 12 169
THE *NEW* ROARING '20S

CHAPTER 13 185
GET A LEGACY

**MEET THE MILLENNIAL
ADVISORY BOARD** 201

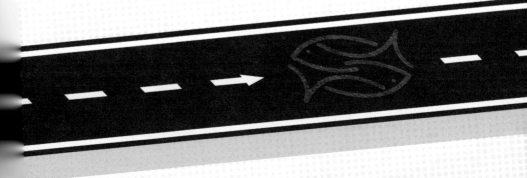

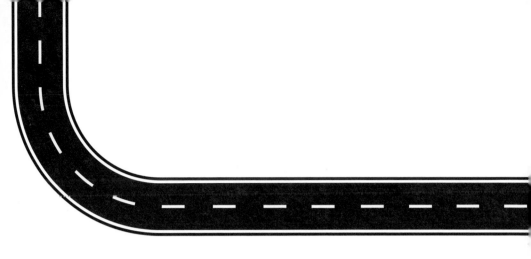

THIS BOOK IS NOT FOR THE TIMID

I'M GOING TO be saying that so many times in the following pages you might get sick of reading it. That's perfectly okay. Because if you do get sick of it, stop reading right now. Why? Because *This Book Is Not for the Timid*. I can't put it any more bluntly than that.

The first two things you need to wrap your head around before diving into *Get a Life* are the following:

This Book Is Not for the Timid.

Life's Too Short.

If that second thing sounds like a weird statement to make at a time when longevity is playing the long game—with more people enjoying productive lives into their 90s—then you just may be too timid to appreciate the rest of what you're about to read. *And This Book Is Not for the Timid.*

No matter how long you live, you will feel that life's too short if you make the most of every minute of every day. That doesn't mean you can't take plenty of time to lean back, rest, and enjoy it fully.

It means that if you make the most of what life can offer, you'll want to do more, and you'll feel that there is always more to do but not always enough time to do it. *This Book Is Not for the Timid.* This book is for the *Obsessed*.

That's where the short part comes in. When you're *Obsessed*, you'll want to accomplish so much, time will seem to speed by, and you'll want the twenty-four hours we have each day to be twenty-five or thirty. If you live each day as if it is too short, then it makes sense to think the same thing about life, which simply is a series of days.

HAVE IT ALL FIGURED OUT?

Why would you want to read this book? It's easier for me to answer "Why would you *not* want to read this book?" I'll tell you why you wouldn't. If you have everything figured out for today and tomorrow and for the rest of your whole life.

If that's you, good luck! I look forward to reading your book on how you figured it out. Until then, though, welcome to my book. *This Book Is Not for the Timid.* It's for the *Fearless*.

This is my second book. Whether you read *Fisch Tales: The Making of a Millennial Baby Boomer* or not won't diminish the value I am confident you will get from reading *Get a Life: A Roadmap to Rule the World*.

They make complementary companions but also stand alone, so you come out ahead either way. You even can read them in reverse—first *Get a Life*, then *Fisch Tales*.

The first words in my first book are "This is not a memoir." Neither is this book. *Fisch Tales* used actual experiences from my long career in retailing to "shed light on how to get the most out of your work life and personal life."

Get a Life picks up where *Fisch Tales* left off. I am still deeply involved in retailing but in a different way from when I ran large companies, including specialty apparel retailer *rue21*, which I took from bankruptcy to a $1 billion valuation with 1,200 stores.

Today I'm super busy being the CEO of my life. Just like I took charge at *rue21*, that's how I run my life—by taking charge. I don't know any other way.

By the way, if you're the kind of retired where it's all play and no work, see ya later! *This Book Is Not for the Timid.*

A GOOD FIT

I sit on the Board of Directors of discount store chain *Ollie's Bargain Outlet* and on the Foundation Board of *Fashion Institute of Technology (FIT)*, where I also mentor, lecture, and manage the *Bob Fisch Graduate Student Award Program* that presents multiple scholarships, entrepreneurial awards, and grants.

I also convene a monthly meeting of my *Millennial Advisory Board (MAB)*, which has contributed to both of my books in very meaningful ways.

Get a Life expands on *Fisch Tales* in a couple of ways. What I mean by *Your Roadmap to Rule the World* as the subtitle is not that this is a manual for global dominance. I'm talking about *Ruling the World* that you create for *Yourself.* It's another way of saying something we've all heard before—that you are the *Master of Your Fate.* Nobody else is. Only you. The bolder your *Ideas* and your

Ambitions, the more you'll come across naysayers who will tell you it can't be done or that you're kidding yourself. I have three words of advice there: *Ignore the Naysayers!* I can also boil that down to two words: Screw them! Instead, do **Whatever It Takes**.

Learn to know who you are, who you want to be, and how you're going to get there. **Learn Not to Be Timid. Take a Stand.**

I am all about taking action, so it's no coincidence that the title of this book begins with an action word. I didn't title it "Have a Nice Life" for a reason. That's passive. Before you *have*, you've got to *get*.

RULES OF REINVENTION

Another way this book has its own *Identity* is that it focuses on **Reinvention** … mine and yours. **Fisch Tales** interspersed **School of Fisch Lessons** within its chapters, helping you "get the most out of your work life and personal life."

In **Get a Life**, each chapter ends with its own **Rules of Reinvention**, advising you how to take your future to a new level—how to supercharge it—by creating a more potent and productive version of **You**.

That's one of the recurring themes of **Get a Life**—creating a stronger **Identity** for yourself.

You'll learn about the importance of **Personal Values, Tribal Knowledge, Vision, Finding Your Calling, Legacy, Mentoring**, and a lot more.

The **Rules** reflect back in their own way on my previous book through the use of the **Fisch Tales** logo as reader-friendly markers. It's the same reason we doubled down in **Get a Life** on the liberal use of italicized, boldfaced key words to pop them out so they stick with you and become an integral part of your self-improvement vocabulary.

Where *Fisch Tales* concentrated on what I learned in my career and passed lessons from that on to the reader, *Get a Life* talks to you, the reader, directly about how to build a life that exceeds your own expectations. I know it can be done because I've done it. And I help others do it, some of whom you'll meet as you journey through the book's *Roadmap*.

I've reinvented myself in the years since I left *rue21*, and I've never felt more fulfilled. That's what I want for you as well. Fulfillment. *Reinvention* is in no way limited by age. You can be a *Baby Boomer* or a *Millennial* or *Gen X* or *Gen Z*. Wanting to *Reinvent* yourself is a state of mind, not a function of age. Be *Fearless*.

As with *Fisch Tales*, my *MAB* once again is showcased with their own section of full-page profiles. We've taken it one step further too. After you learn a little about each member of *MAB*, it's your turn to dive in and create your own profile page. So start thinking about what *Obsesses* you, what one *Word* defines you, and who is your *Alter Ego*, which are some of the fun yet revealing ways to explore the *You* inside *You*.

FOCUS ON YOUR FUTURE

I reinvented myself several times in the course of my career. I didn't do it to seek the best-paying jobs for the money. That's not how I define success. In fact, I once turned down a job that offered considerably more money because I was convinced that staying where I was—for less money—offered the best *Future* for me. That's another running theme of *Get a Life*. Focus on the *Future* because when you look in the rearview mirror at the other end, how you manage your future today determines what your *Legacy* looks like tomorrow.

If you go chasing money for its own sake, you are timid. ***And This Book Is Not for the Timid.*** Money is the incidental reward, not the destination. Searching only for the big bucks means you're not searching inside yourself first to figure out the meaning of your existence, not only what it means to you but also to others.

It's not about the money, and it's not about becoming famous. Would you rather be a celebrity for the shallow sake of fame or be good at what you do? If it's superficial fame you want, that's timid too. ***And This Book Is Not for the Timid.***

I have concerns. That's another reason I wrote ***Get a Life***. I'm concerned that not enough people I mentor or casually meet push enough to make things happen. Of course I mean to make things happen for yourself. But when you do that, you also can make good things happen for others. More than ever, we have to watch out for each other.

If you're at a hotel or a restaurant and you experience poor customer service, you can choose to say nothing, and that same experience will be repeated for other patrons. Or you can speak up to a manager, not to make a scene but to make your feelings known. That could help improve the experience for others who come after you.

THE MODES OF MENTORING

In that way, my intention is that the answers in this book on how to manage situations in your life will give you answers you don't get every day. This book will help you get there.

In my experience at ***FIT***, I have found that students are starved for ***Mentoring***—all the forms of it I list in this book—***Mutual Mentoring, Mental Mentoring, Motivational Mentoring***. That's part of the ***Intergenerational Bonding*** I practice with those I ***Mentor*** of other generations. ***I Teach Them Business. They Teach Me Life!***

When I started thinking about and researching for **Get a Life**, there were many questions that popped into my head. They are the questions I hear from young people. I have no doubt, since you are reading this book right now, that they are questions you ask yourself.

Such questions as …

What is the seed of success?

When did you first feel successful?

How do you create your own niche?

How do you channel your desire to achieve your dreams?

How do you motivate yourself?

Have you experienced fear of success?

How far ahead do you visualize your life?

How do you give back?

What do you want to be remembered for?

How you answer those questions tells me how far you want to go in life. Every day should build on the one that came before it. You're not competing with anybody other than yourself.

This Book Is Not for the Timid. It is not for people who are satisfied with being ordinary. It's not for people who are worried about so-called **Work-Life Balance**. Give me a break! **Work-Life Balance** is nothing but word salad. It's meaningless.

WORK-LIFE INTEGRATION

If you are looking for balance, go buy a scale. Those who succeed don't obsess over something as timid as **Work-Life Balance**. It's just a way of saying "I can't wait to get off of work to live my life." Huh? I don't talk that language.

If your work is not an integral part of your life, then you don't have a **Calling**. This book will help you understand the meaning of

7

that as well as the difference between *Calling* and *Job*. *Work-Life Integration Is for the Fearless. Work-Life Balance Is for the Timid. This Book Is Not for the Timid.*

One of the worst pieces of advice you could follow in your job or your career is to *Stay in Your Lane*. My wife, *Stephanie*, overheard in a park two people talking. One told the other that she ended up doing some of her boss's work because the boss was not doing it. When she told her boss about the situation, she was told to not do work that belonged to her boss. Just let the boss fail on her own. In other words, the worker was told to *Stay in Her Lane*!

That's the opposite of what I would tell that person. You serve your company best by making sure you help wherever you can. There are no lanes. In letting your boss fail, you are failing your company. I don't recognize lanes. Neither should you. Lanes are for the timid. *And This Book Is Not for the Timid.*

I started work on this book in the middle of the pandemic, which only has made what I have to say even more timely—and necessary. We're now living in a post-pandemic world that is unlike anything we have known in our lifetime and that will influence the rest of our lives and those of future generations. That's not my opinion, just an obvious fact.

THE NEW NORMAL

Consider the phrase *Mental Health*. Not very long ago, those words had a real stigma attached to them. Today it's a common malady we all can relate to and may confront more frequently than ever, in ourselves or in others close to us.

It used to be we rarely would hear about so-called "air rage" incidents. In a typical year, there would be about 150 incidents reported of people behaving badly on commercial flights. In 2021 there were more than five *thousand* air rage incidents reported!

In a post-pandemic society, we all need each other more than ever, and that requires one of the most important words in **Get a Life—Empathy**. The pandemic is the strongest reminder we could get that the world around us is in a constant state of change. That's all the more reason we need to train ourselves to stay constant within the confines of our personal world and not get swept up in the never-ending changes that are a constant in the outside world.

My worldview is that life is full of contradictions, and the more we acknowledge and accept that, the better we can manage our lives. You may think discipline, for instance, is inhibiting. But it's the opposite—liberating. You may think being a **Disruptor** is bad. But it's not. It's trying to improve things. Being an **Interruptor** is bad. It's trying to prevent improvement.

As I was writing this, it was reported that the world's oldest person, 119 years old, had passed. The next oldest in line were 116 and 115. So buckle up and enjoy the ride because you've got a long way to go, baby, and **The Best Is Yet to Come**!

HELLO, THIS IS YOUR CAREER CALLING

ARE YOU WORKING TO LIVE or living to work? That's how a member of my *Millennial Advisory Board (MAB)*, *Nicole Campbell*, likes to put it. If you only are working at your Job to live—paycheck to paycheck—you have neither a *Calling* nor much of a Career.

If, however, you are living to work—and, of course, to enjoy the fruits of your labor—you have a shot at finding your true *Calling* and converting it into a long and memorable Career.

In other words, you should be doing *both*—living to work and working to live.

We all know about Careers and Jobs, but that terminology is changing, along with the modern workforce. In the United States, at the end of 2022, *Millennials* and *Gen Z* comprised 150 million people or nearly half—45 percent—of the population. Those generations think in terms of Gigs and Freelance and Side Hustles as well as Jobs and Careers.

The notion of having a one-track Career—a decades-long haul in the same industry, if not the same company—is now officially quaint.

We've traveled from the twentieth-century tradition of gold watches presented to retiring forty-year employees to twenty-first-century smart watches sported by twenty-five-year-old solopreneurs.

A Job is a single unit that exists in a frozen moment in time. It's not a Career strategy in and of itself, and if you think of it as a mere Job, it certainly is not a *Calling*.

A Job is a holding pattern while you figure out your next move, and the one after that, and after that. The proverbial Career ladder. The *Pieces of the Puzzle*.

You need to constantly be working at *what* you want, *how much* you want it, and *how* to get it. Thinking in Job terms is short-term thinking. Even if you love what you do, the question you need to ask yourself is, "Where is this job taking me?" You *should* be restless. You *should* be **Relentless**. That's your **Ambition** nagging you. Don't ignore it!

Dione O'Dell, another member of my **MAB**, didn't ignore her **Ambition**. She's a very special person who **Put It on the Line** by opening a boutique clothing store—during the pandemic! Now that's what I call a *Calling*. Not even a historic public health crisis was going to stop her from following her **Obsession** all the way through to reaching her goal.

Dione rose up through the ranks at **rue21** to become vice president of marketing. Among her many qualities is that she not only has uncanny instincts and wisdom but Dione also applies her smarts with efficient productivity. She knows how to **Execute**.

In August 2021, after six months of intensive planning, Dione opened The Gardenia Branch store, "a super trendy fashion boutique designed for women of all ages," in Pittsburgh's Ross Park Mall.

"Opening during the pandemic in a world going through so many changes and ups and downs is something that I wanted to take the risk to do," she told me. "Following my gut made me want to just go for it."

It would have been easy for Dione to hide in a *Comfort Zone* and not take such a big, bold risk. But that's not her. Instead, she rose up to meet the challenge and pursue her dream. That's what a *Calling* compels us to do.

INVITE CHALLENGES

What does it take to be successful and to get ahead in the midst of performing a job? To me, it means not only accepting challenges but also *welcoming* challenges. Only by doing that can you keep reaching higher, improve your skills, outhustle your competition (within the company) who is vying for the same promotion, and satisfy the customer (your boss).

> How you behave and perform in any single Job determines not only the quality of your next job but also the trajectory and velocity of your Career.

How you behave and perform in any single Job determines not only the quality of your next job but also the trajectory and velocity of your Career. If you are Job-hopping (advancing from one position to the next) in the belief that it equals a Career, you're doing it backward. First, you need to decide what kind of

Career you want. No, strike that. You need to decide what kind of *Life* you want.

We need to stop thinking in terms of a Career comprising a series of Jobs that are similar to each other, with the main difference of earning added responsibilities along the way.

That's self-defeating, constricting, and not very imaginative. It limits the possibilities. A Career doesn't need to be linear. It can go off in different directions at different times or even at the same time. That's why the word Career is not fully in tune with these times.

Where does a *Calling* come in then? That's harder to pin down. And not everybody necessarily has a *Calling*. Or knows that they have one. How do you find that out?

Here's one way to explain it.

Imagine yourself an eight-year-old who has no doubt that you will grow into a famous performer. A lot of us have those fantasies as young children. President! A superstar on a stage or in a sports stadium! Astronaut!

"THE BOSS" KNEW HE'D BE BOSS

For most of us, what we end up being is a far cry from what we imagined ourselves becoming.

There are exceptions, though. Those who know exactly what they want then go out and get it. And make it *big*.

Let's talk *Bruce Springsteen*.

The rock legend told the story in his one-man Broadway show of the *Calling* that visited him—like a guardian angel—at a very young age.

He had every *Confidence*, from that point forward, that his fantastic *Vision* for himself would find fulfillment. Having *Confi-*

dence in yourself cannot be overstated. It is what enables *Dominance* and *Success*.

Is a *Calling* some kind of metaphysical gift only a lucky few inherit, like a fortune, or win, like a lottery?

Or is a *Calling* a sixth sense telling you who you are meant to be, reinforced by *Confidence* and a hunger to constantly up your game?

It's both.

A *Calling* calls for you to be many things. *Obsessed* and *Fearless* are two of the things.

I am not saying that a *Calling* is obtainable only to an elite few. For some, it appears sooner and with less effort than for others. For those to whom it does not come easily, you can't conjure a *Calling* by snapping your fingers or waving a magic wand. A *Calling* is born somewhere inside you. It's not like searching for a Job. You don't find it. *It finds you.* You can invite it in if you are receptive to it.

It's not important where it came from or how it got there.

BE ALERT FOR SIGNALS

What's important is that you recognize it when you see it, when it touches you and forges your outlook on how best to fulfill your destiny. It's an aching *Ambition* that burns within you. It must be quenched. That's a *Signal* to watch for. (As you'll see in chapter 2, I believe in *Signals* and its twin, *Timing*.)

When the legendary life that would be his *Calling* came for Bruce Springsteen, he was in grade school. Even at that tender age, he had outsize *Ambition*. Being *Ambitious* is another essential ingredient of acting out your *Calling*. To be clear, recognizing a *Calling* at such a young age is not at all typical, and it is not to be expected. It's just another way in which Springsteen is one of a kind.

When that visitation of a *Calling* happened to me, I was a graduate student in marriage counseling at *Columbia University*. I didn't think of that profession as my *Calling*, mind you, but as a Career.

What's the difference? A *Calling*—think of it as a *Signal* or *Epiphany*—takes inspiration. A Career—the ability to spin gold from your *Calling* to make it self-sustaining—takes perspiration.

A *Calling* is similar to having a *Vision*. But once it presents itself to you, a *Vision* must be achieved, or it remains ephemeral, without substance or direction.

It's not a free ride to get there. You have to pave your own road and pay your own way. Not with asphalt and money but with *Grit* and *Sweat* and *Ingenuity* and *Ambition* and *Confidence*—and *Passion*.

The right person(s) giving you timely and strategic guidance can have a profound influence on who you become. One of my most memorable mentors did nothing less than literally change the direction my life took.

Improbably, I owe my *Calling* as a retail innovator to a marriage counselor. He was an author and a teacher at *Columbia University—Dr. Paul Vahanian*, who was my advisor there.

More important, he was my trusted *Mentor*. Having one is no less important than having *Vision*, *Passion*, *Ambition*, and *Confidence*.

DON'T SETTLE FOR YOUR SECOND CHOICE

At one meeting, Dr. Vahanian asked me what I wanted to do with my life. I said that I wasn't positive that I wanted to be a marriage counselor. I just didn't know what other Career to choose at that time. It wasn't so much that marriage counseling was my first choice. It was my default choice. *Not* a good sign.

The next words out of my *Mentor*'s mouth made all the difference in the world I would create and inhabit for the next four-plus decades.

"I don't think you should be a marriage counselor. It's not for you."

What might have sounded to another person like a put-down was music to my ears! It was the *Signal*. If this guy's a marriage counselor himself and he can see that's not a *Passion* that burns in me, how much more of a *Signal* did I need?

That may be my personal *Calling* story, but there's an object lesson in there for anyone reading this: If you choose your Career as I initially did—without genuine *Passion*—I urge you to rethink that choice. It's not too late. I don't believe it's ever too late to rethink your options and do what is best for you. *The Best Is Yet to Come.*

That's exactly what I did, and it made all the difference in my life. Instead of marriage counseling, my professional life was kick-started as an executive trainee at premier department store *Abraham & Straus (A&S)*. My journey culminated as the founding CEO of *rue21*, which, by 2014, I had built into the largest specialty apparel retailer, by store count (1,200), in America.

FREEDOM TO BE YOURSELF

What I experienced the first day at A&S was an *Epiphany* for me. I was excited by the enjoyment and *Confidence* it gave me to be in such a dynamic environment. I had found something where I had the freedom to be myself.

Just as making music was for eight-year-old Bruce Springsteen, for twenty-three-year-old *Bob Fisch*, it was clear as could be that the business world of retailing was my **Calling**. It was meant to be. We were made for each other.

That's also how I would describe almost every Job I've ever held in my Career.

Where do **Calling**, Career, and Job intersect or diverge?

Springsteen had **Passion**, **Vision**, and **Confidence**. So did I. What about you?

Yet even those alone are not enough, I'm afraid. You'd be hard-pressed to meet almost any serious musician who does *not* exude genuine **Passion** about their craft.

Then what is it that separates the general run of musicians possessed by that **Calling** from the pantheon of supernovas like Bruce Springsteen?

It's undeniable that a Springsteen-size talent has a mystical muse that speaks in a unique way not only to him but also to his legions of fans.

For creative artists, a **Calling** fed by a muse that resonates with the general public—crafting songs like Springsteen's or best sellers like **Stephen King**'s—is the stuff that dreams are made of.

So if the muse (inspiration) feeds the **Calling**, what feeds the muse?

Work Ethic!

The muse needs to be constantly exercised. It needs ongoing stimulation to create an instant classic like Springsteen's *Born to Run* or King's *The Shining*.

THE IMPORTANCE OF PERSEVERANCE

To galvanize your **Calling** into a successful Career takes a tremendous amount of **Perseverance**. There's a distinction to recognize between a **Calling** that's pre-ordained and a Career that's richly rewarding, both spiritually and financially. Remember, one is organic (*Calling*), while the other must be built from scratch (Career).

In between those points A and Z is a sizable gap you have to fill with a plan and with a *Relentless* pursuit of excellence.

Someone who has impressed me greatly with his *Work Ethic*, his *Vision*, and how he has managed his *Calling* is *Adam Witty*. He's the Founder and Chief Executive Officer of *Forbes Books*, the company that published both my books as well as thousands of others.

While still in his early twenties, Adam's *Vision* was not necessarily to become only a publishing house. He called his overall concept *Authority Marketing*. Books, like the two I've authored, are one part of Adam's concept. Other parts include speaking engagements, podcasts, blogs, websites, and anything else that helps brand and package authority for a targeted segment of the public.

Adam and I are like mirror images of each other when it comes to our views on how to *Get a Life*.

Take our dismissal of work-life balance. "To me, it's all just a living," he told me. "If you really love what you do and see what you do as a *Calling*, it isn't work versus play. It all merges together. There's a *Mark Twain* quote that the object of life is to make your vocation your vacation, and I never forgot that one."

Hear also what Adam has to say about another kind of balance: where you work.

"To truly turn a career into a *Calling*, there are interpersonal relationships and communications that are developed with people. It's a lot harder to do virtually. It's not as effective. I'm not anti-work-from-home, but I think there is a balance in person where you can collaborate, communicate, and integrate with other people and have human connections, not just through a screen. That goes a long way toward ultimately helping people have much higher career satisfaction."

Adam believes that while everybody has a calling, "very few people ever discover it." He blames the pressure that society places on us. "Some people pursue fields or careers because they think they should instead of because they really want to, or the rationale goes that 'My parents and grandparents were doctors, so that's what I *need* to be.'"

I've had a lot of good fortune in my Career. What about luck? It doesn't hurt to have benefited along the way from some lucky breaks when the **Timing** was right for a decision I made, but I believe you make your own luck. I had to recognize when the **Timing** worked to our advantage and then take advantage of it. To do that, you need to be at the top of your game every minute of every day. That's not luck. That's **Discipline** and **Focus**.

It's not to say that I'm not grateful for how things have worked out for me through the years. It leaves you humble that you were able to make the right decisions more often than not.

If you treat it right, if you nurture it properly and zealously, a *Calling* lifts you to new levels and brings into view far-reaching horizons.

A *Calling* blurs the line between your professional life and your personal life, and that is as good as it gets because if it feels too much like work, it's not so much a *Calling* as a Job.

> **If you treat it right, if you nurture it properly and zealously, a *Calling* lifts you to new levels and brings into view far-reaching horizons.**

I don't believe thirty-year-olds should be wasting time and energy fretting about "work-life balance." Just do well for yourself and your coworkers, and the balance will come.

I love Adam Witty's perspective and the way he articulates it. "To me, it's really work-life purpose. If you find purpose, or *Calling*, it integrates with your life. If you work eighty hours a week and you love what you do and find purpose in it, then you're in balance." *Yes! Exactly!*

TIME-STAMP YOUR GOALS

Instead of waking up one day in middle age to wonder, "Why haven't I fulfilled my *Ambition*?" set goals now. Write down a goal as soon as you think of it, or it will disappear into thin air. Put a date on the goal. Hold yourself accountable to each goal and to your future self!

Think how crazy it sounds to wake up on that day, years from now, and tell yourself, "Well, I'm not where I want to be professionally, but at least my work-life balance is really good." So what? It's meaningless.

That's backward thinking. Stop worrying about the balance. Do the work to the best of your ability. Enrich yourself through work, and the enrichment will multiply in other parts of your life.

If you work hard at doing what you enjoy and make a sufficient income, your life organically will seek its natural balance.

The key to getting there is *Consistency*. You need to sustain it for a long time, but it's achievable if you fix your focus squarely on today. Each day brings its own fresh chance for success and improvement.

Think how gratifying it will be years from now when you look back and appreciate how your day-to-day consistency added up to a meaningful life you can savor rather than regret.

Some people think being a workaholic is a *Calling*. It's not. The very word "workaholic" tells you it's not truly a *Calling*. It's being inefficient. It's emphasizing quantity over quality. It's pushing yourself to the limit. A *Calling* feels like there is no limit. It feels frictionless.

There also is no quota on *Callings*. Even now, as a follow-up to my original *Calling* in retailing, I'm fully engaged and fully enjoying playing out another *Calling*, in conjunction with *FIT* in New York City. Working with *FIT* President *Dr. Joyce Brown*, I'm giving back by paying it forward through *Mentoring*, scholarships, and other contributions that support the school and its graduate students.

BUILDING A BRAND

As I see it, my role at *FIT* is not only to give back in various ways but also to serve as a role model for other board members to do the same. It's building a brand and a platform to help students and the school, where my Vision is clear to see, enabling others to easily emulate the *Mentoring* model.

At *FIT*, I serve on the foundation board, an advisory and fundraising body of the college. Five years before I came on board, when I was CEO of *rue21*, I had been a guest lecturer and advisor for the Fashion Merchandising Capstone Project that *FIT* senior students undertake.

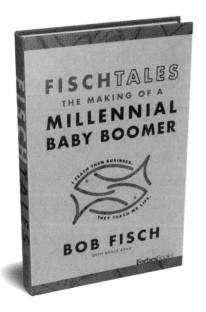

My emphasis was on the *Mutual Mentoring* and *Reverse Mentoring* strategy outlined in my book *Fisch Tales: The Making of a Millennial Baby Boomer* (Forbes Books).

That gratifying experience became the basis for my second *Calling*. (There's no word in my vocabulary that begins with "retire-" and ends with "-ment." That's nonnegotiable.)

At *FIT*, I established a $300,000 endowment known as the ***Bob Fisch Graduate Student Award Program***. It includes an Entrepreneurial Excellence Award, Thesis Project Completion grants, and scholarships for *FIT*'s ***Fashion Design MFA*** and ***Global Fashion Management MPS*** programs.

My *FIT* role has rewarded me anew. It is a fitting way to extend and enhance my career in retailing through all of the above activities, plus a series of Fireside Chats that I have with graduate students as well as holding one-to-one mentoring sessions.

It's true that I've given a financial gift to *FIT* and its students, but a ***Calling*** is in its own way, like a gift to yourself. How you develop and use the gift is how you transform a ***Calling*** into a Career and a ***Legacy*** (see ***chapter 13***).

Ask yourself, What are the ***Signals*** that point me toward the gift I want to give myself? What is it I love to do that would nurture the rest of my life?

Now what are you going to do with that gift?

Bob Fisch and FIT President Dr. Joyce Brown congratulate students receiving the Bob Fisch Entrepreneurial Award.

RULES OF REINVENTION

IS THAT CALL FOR YOU?

- A *Calling* means you have a sixth sense about what you want to do with your life.

- A *Calling* does *not* mean that you can go on autopilot to galvanize your Calling into a great Career. Think of a *Calling* as a gift you've given yourself. It's what you do with the gift that determines its long-term value.

- A *Calling* takes inspiration. A Career takes perspiration.

- You can succeed whether or not you believe your Career is a *Calling*. Don't let a Career happen to you. You need to make it happen to your specifications and to your liking.

- A Job is one step along the journey, not a destination. If your job is mainly a practical way to earn a paycheck but does not prepare you for advancement, move on. That impatience and frustration and ambition nagging at you is your Career calling. Be ready to answer the *Call*.

- Work-Life Balance is what *Results* when you are *Disciplined* and *Farsighted* about managing your *Calling* or your Career day-to-day. The Balance is the *Result* you must earn, not a predetermined means to an end.

- Be alert and respond to *Signals*. If a new opportunity or a new Career direction presents itself, explore it. The *Timing* may not be as good later on as it is right now.

- It's never too late to make a switch in your Job, your Career, your Life! Regardless of your age, adopt the mantra I live by— *The Best Is Yet to Come*.

IT'S ALL IN
THE TIMING

WHEN I LEFT CASUAL CORNER after a new owner wanted to take it in a different direction from where I wanted to take the company, I wasn't sure what would come next in my career. I looked at plenty of possibilities, but nothing clicked for me.

What I want you to know—and remember—is that I had *put* myself in a position where I didn't have to take the first new thing that came along or even the second thing. Through connections I had made at the right time, I had offers. Whether or not they were right for me is beside the point. The point is I had choices for me to decide on. To be clear, I did not *find* myself in that positive position—I *placed* myself there by everything I had done to that point. That's a huge distinction.

That's the first lesson in this chapter on *Timing* and *Signals*: Make it your business to have a fallback position, where you might have to make concessions before you get what you want. If you find yourself looking for new career opportunities and the Timing isn't to your liking for the first thing that comes along, I don't want you to feel forced to settle for the wrong opportunity.

Recognizing the **Signals** and taking advantage of opportunities at the right time requires powers of concentration, discipline, and sweat equity. You have to fight for what you want, and if you make a compelling case that you are right, people will be inclined to give you what you want. Good **Timing** happens when you take action and force others to react to you.

I've always been careful about watching out for myself that way. I'm not about to let anyone get the upper hand with me. Whatever I do in life or career, it's because I want to do it, not because I am being forced by someone else or by circumstances to do it. What about you? Are you in full control of your fate? If not, take control!

Wherever I worked—*A&S*, *Jordan Marsh*, *Casual Corner*, *rue21*—I did it my way. When I was recommended for the formidable job of taking over **Pennsylvania Fashions** (which I would remake into *rue21*), I was ready for any challenge.

Had I passed up that offer, all signs were that the company would have disappeared. That's what the owners wanted to do: shut it down. If I didn't take the job, I wouldn't have disappeared, but I highly doubt that my next career move, whatever it might have been, would have come anywhere close to matching the turnaround and subsequent high-flying success we achieved at *rue21*, steering it from chapter 11 bankruptcy to a valuation over $1 billion.

YOU MAKE TIMING HAPPEN

You might look at that dramatic turning point in my career and think, "What great *Timing*, Bob!" As if it's something good that *happened to* me. Wrong! I can't emphasize enough that it's something good I *made* happen. All the moves I had made in my career leading up to that point are what enabled the Timing to work in my favor. It's all connected. Timing may look or feel arbitrary. Don't be fooled. It's not. It's what I call **Pieces of the Puzzle**, and you're in charge of putting it together to form a full, and fulfilling, picture. Is that how you view your life?

What excited me about **rue21** was the chance to prove I could beat the odds against turning around a massively failing business. That's what gets my juices going. I call it the **Art of the Possible**. What gets *you* jazzed? Do you have your own impossible you want to conquer?

I already had started to build a successful value business at Casual Corner, but my progress was cut short by the new owner. That frustration served as a **Signal** to me that Pennsylvania Fashions presented another opportunity to continue proving my value-priced fashion retail concept, with stores in strip malls and not just outlet centers.

Was the *Timing* for a turnaround—both in my career and at my new company—pointing in my favor? Yes, but only because of everything that I made happen to that point. I'm not unique that way. I just realize that while *Timing* may seem like it's an

> While *Timing* may seem like it's an external force that works for us or against us, in reality, it's more in our control than we think.

27

external force that works for us or against us, in reality, it's more in our control than we think.

Your everyday decisions and long-term life strategy all play into what we call *Timing*. You need to be more aware of the role you play in *Timing* to optimize its positive effects on your life. Set yourself up to make that happen, and take advantage of it. I am very cognizant of how *Signals* and *Timing* lead my life. What about you?

I can't emphasize enough also that *Timing* is not about getting lucky. Luck is make-believe. You must continually put yourself in a position to make your own luck. That's the only kind of luck that you can count on because you control the outcome, not some mysterious force.

How your personal decisions and behavior affect your career is an example of internal *Timing* that is unique to you. What's important is that you recognize it when you see it, when it touches you and forges your outlook on how best to fulfill your destiny. It's an aching ambition that burns within you. It must be quenched. Ask yourself every day, what time is it in my life, what am I going to do with it, and where will it take me?

RIGHT TIME FOR START-UPS

There also are factors of external *Timing* that affect many people all at the same time. For instance, a pandemic.

Do you know which year set a record for the most business start-ups in the United States?

In 2020, the first year that COVID-19 disrupted all our lives, there were a record-setting 4.4-plus million new U.S. businesses created (according to the Census Bureau).

The upsurge in entrepreneurship during hard times is nothing new. It's a matter of fact that recessions are hotbeds of invention and innovation. The roll call of companies created during the eighteen-month Great Recession (December 2007–June 2009) reads like a Who's Who of twenty-first-century tech stocks: WhatsApp, Groupon, Venmo, Uber.

During the pandemic especially, it's not hard to see what was so appealing about starting your own business. Working from home meant you could work on your dream project any time of day. People also had more time and energy to invest in side hustles without the commute to and from work.

It also meant the dramatic upheaval in lifestyles created new opportunities, like food delivery apps and services and home-baked goods to take advantage of the whole farm-to-table, organic, healthy food movement. People also had time to explore new markets, like podcasts, that weren't practical in the prepandemic world.

That external kind of **Timing** is easy to recognize. It's hard *not* to see. Nobody with a pulse could possibly miss the **Signals** that the pandemic triggered, leading to perfect **Timing** for so many opportunities that hadn't existed—or weren't as obvious—before 2020.

That's not how it works in everyday life, though. **Signals** can be tricky things to notice. You have to pay close attention and be on the lookout. They normally don't announce themselves as loudly as the pandemic did.

Sometimes a **Signal** could be telling you what *not* to do.

In 2011 the **Cotton Crisis** rocked the soft goods industry, causing supply-chain spikes in price. It sent a predictable **Signal** to retailers to pass along the price increase to their customers. That's the way those things typically work.

COMPETITIVE STRATEGY

I'm not interested in being typical, and neither should you be. The *Cotton Crisis* sent me a very different *Signal*. It made me realize what better *Timing* than when all our competitors were raising prices than to dig in our heels and lock in our existing prices.

We told our suppliers we weren't budgeted to pay them any more than what we already were paying. With *rue21* ordering some items in the millions of units, they weren't about to write off our business. As a result, they did not raise their prices to us, and we didn't raise our prices to customers.

We came out of the *Cotton Crisis* as one of a handful of retailers who weren't financially damaged by it, while some other retailers continued to feel the adverse effects for years to come.

That's what it's like to recognize *Signals* and *Opportunities* on a large scale. The pandemic and *Cotton Crisis* were as obvious as *Signals* get. More often than not, the *Timing* and *Signals* I talk about happen on a much more personal level.

It doesn't get more personal than the kind of *Signal* that is so overwhelming in its negativity people who receive it question whether they ever will recover from the impact. Yet, if handled the right way, those same devastating *Signals* can ultimately inspire and influence your *Timing*.

My lifelong friend lost his fifteen-year-old son because of a medical condition. The boy's twelve-year-old sister, seeing her normally upbeat father in an unrecognizable state of depression, asked her mother, "Will Daddy ever be happy again?"

As grief-stricken as he was by the unthinkable *Signal* he and his wife just had been dealt, when he heard the innocent and poignant question his daughter asked his wife, that was the *Signal* to gain strength from their loss and to quickly turn it into something that would lift his daughter, honor her brother's memory, and give them renewed purpose. The *Timing* told them to start a charity in their son's name.

It's also possible—and at times crucial—to send yourself a *Signal*. It might be telling yourself it's not the right time to do something you are very passionate about.

That happened with the ***Miami Heat*** of the National Basketball Association. I've had season tickets at their arena for more than thirty years. I very much want to become involved with their great organization. That's why I reached out to them—to explore the best way I can mentor their interns as well as students at colleges that are associated with the Heat.

TIME MANAGEMENT

As those talks were in progress, my involvement with *FIT* gained momentum. There were *Signals* at work there too that resulted in the *FIT Timing* working out as I wanted.

There were many moving pieces to manage in creating *FIT*'s ***Bob Fisch Graduate Student Award Program***. That's not unusual when coming to terms on an agreement, whether it's a deal in the corporate world or in the world of academia. The process took quite a while, in part because I pay close attention to details.

One of the moving parts was that *FIT* asked me to hold meetings with its graduate design and graduate merchandising classes. During the pandemic, though, I did not want to have them on Zoom. It's a great tool that made the pandemic much more bearable and productive. At the same time, video conferencing is no match for the energy and empathy and spontaneity of being in the same room with everyone.

By the time everything was resolved between **FIT** and me, students were permitted to return to in-person classes. That allowed **FIT** President **Dr. Joyce Brown** to make the announcement *in person* of the scholarship program at the very start of the fall 2021 school term.

The **Timing** was right on the money for the school to get what it needed and for me to get what I wanted by holding in-person group mentoring conversations with the students.

While all that was evolving, the Miami Heat proposed a mentoring relationship with me. I held off on developing that idea further, though, because, with **FIT** fully in play, the **Timing** was not ideal to proceed with the Heat.

If I can't devote my full attention to an ambitious project like that, it's a **Signal** that I need to wait until the **Timing** feels just right. That's an example of how **Hesitancy** can be a **Signal**. Do you trust your instincts? It's important not to get stressed in taking on more than you can handle comfortably.

CLOSE ENCOUNTERS

You can have fun with **Timing** too, using it to indulge a passion and at the same time give yourself a playful challenge. On a business trip to Las Vegas years ago, I happened to know Miami Heat basketball star **Dwyane Wade** would be staying at the same hotel as me—the Wynn. I was convinced that I'd meet up with him in an elevator. Not because I believe in coincidences but because I was determined to will it to happen.

I pride myself on making things happen, whether it's business or pleasure. Sure enough, Dwyane walked by, with **LeBron James** no less. He entered the elevator car, and I followed him. "Good to see you, Dwyane," I said. It may seem like a small thing to you, but to me, I had a blast just making that moment come true.

Whether it's business or pleasure, my reason for telling you that story is to illustrate how you can will something to happen, because you can.

If it wasn't for the *Signal* that moving on from *rue21* provided, I might never have joined with *FIT* or published two books, through my affiliation with Forbes Books. The career change turned into a clear *Signal* to go do something else with my life.

As I was leaving *rue21*, I naturally wondered how it would affect my life. What would I do, sit back or lean forward? My answer to that question was to get busy planning the next chapters in my life. I didn't realize how leaving *rue21* after fifteen years would turn into a series of timely *Opportunities* for me.

I'm having the time of my life by waking up at the crack of dawn, running five miles on a treadmill nearly every day, and working on my ongoing plans to rule the world. That's what I am compelled to do.

What are you compelled to do with *your* life?

RULES OF REINVENTION

PAY ATTENTION TO TIMING AND SIGNALS

Timing

- Whether it's your career or your life, get it out of your head that *Timing* is something mystical that happens to you. *Timing* is controllable. You make *Timing* happen with every individual action you take in pursuit of a *Goal*.

- There is no such thing as "getting lucky." You create your luck the hard way by earning it with every individual action you take in pursuit of a *Goal*.

- *Timing* is not Good or Bad. Those words wrongly reinforce the misconception that *Timing* is out of your control. Instead, think of *Timing* as Right or Wrong. Those words reinforce the *Truth* that *you* can control the *Timing* of events and decisions in your life and career.

Signals

- A *Signal* is an event or decision point that triggers an action you should take or triggers an action you should not take.

- A *Signal* can be sent to you personally, such as leaving a job.

- A *Signal* can be sent to the general public, such as a pandemic.

- To take advantage of opportunities or to avoid a bad decision, you must stay aware at all times of subtle *Signals* that can affect you personally. In other words, you need to develop a sixth sense for *Signals* that may not be obvious.

- You can turn a *Signal* that seems bad at first into a positive outcome if your attitude is positive and your thinking is creative.

I TEACH THEM BUSINESS, THEY TEACH ME LIFE!

TO CELEBRATE THE NEW YEAR, my wife, *Stephanie*, and I have an annual ritual that has lasted thirty New Years—we spend a few days at the *Ritz-Carlton* in Naples, Florida. It's a golden chance for us to be alone and to relax and for me to free my mind of all the daily details of my work that it is my way to obsess over the rest of the year.

During our respite there, two years into the COVID-19 pandemic, I noticed something had changed. Even when on vacation, I pay close attention to details. I make it a point to get to know all the hotel personnel who can make our experience more comfortable and stress-free.

The hotel recently had reopened. As with so many other businesses, it was a downsized staff. It also was a noticeably less experienced staff. My customer service radar was alerted immediately that I'd have to pay very close attention every step of the way to ensure our expectations were met, as they always had been in the past at this beautiful resort. The Ritz-Carlton brand is synonymous with top-tier amenities and quality of experience.

As we spoke with the newcomers on staff, and as they confided in me, it became clear to me what had changed. They were not receiving the on-the-job training that is necessary to maintain the Ritz-Carlton gold standard.

Even as we were dining, a hotel staffer would share with us her frustrations about not knowing fully what she should be doing or how to do it properly. Now some people in our position, as hotel guests, might find that inappropriate and presumptuous and downright annoying.

But the hotel worker wouldn't be telling us her story unless she sensed that we were receptive to listening—and to helping. That's *Intergenerational Bonding*.

In that situation, and in others like it in my travels, the staffing dilemmas faced by employers during the pandemic resulted in the hiring of workers with limited, or no, skills for the jobs they were given. There emerged a cry for help that I began hearing more frequently—"No one is mentoring me."

New workers were being thrown into a high-pressure position for which they were not fully prepared.

ASK FOR HELP TO HELP YOURSELF

To the Ritz-Carlton people, I urged them to talk to their manager. Be assertive. State your case in a way that tells your supervisor you not only need guidance but also want it because you want to do your job as well as possible. You want to do it as well as possible to help your company look its best. It's far better to acknowledge you need support and advice than to act like you know it all when you don't and then slip up in a way that can get you fired.

A longtime Ritz associate, who'd been there for decades, expressed to me frustration with some of the changes he had been witnessing. I encouraged him to take that frustration to his boss. This is someone who makes a notable difference in the high regard the hotel is held. He has provided the same quality service to three generations of families. You better believe management would take his concerns seriously. But he first had to have the confidence in his own importance to the company. That's what I tried to give him. **Confidence.** That's how progress is made in anything we do.

It's not just about me being on a campaign of encouragement with anybody I come across. Like I'm the Pied Piper of Progress. (Although that's not such a bad handle, come to think of it.) We all should be promoting progress whenever the opportunity arises. If I complain about a person or experience, I don't want them to lose their job. I want them to know what to change to keep their job.

I go out of my way to keep pushing for better results no matter the circumstance, even if it means I need to go out of my way to do it. Not everybody is built exactly like me, but you can adapt it to your personal style and still get results. But going out of your comfort zone has its rewards. You don't need to imitate my hard-driving style. It doesn't work for everybody. It's enough of a step in the right direction if you go out of your way to take chances. Over time, as it begins to feel more natural, you will feel like you have a new superpower!

In another instance during our stay, I made recommendations to managers stemming from an unsatisfactory experience I had in the spa, and they actually adopted my suggestions. The point is not that

I was complaining about a bad situation I encountered but that I was determined, as I always am, to be a change agent. How did I do that? Through *Intergenerational Bonding*.

That's just one example. The bonding of disparate generations can happen anywhere and everywhere, and it does, every day.

It happens when a teacher is interacting with students.

It happens when children visit grandparents in an assisted-living residence.

MAKE AGE A BOND, NOT A BARRIER

In other words, intergenerational bonding has been around quite a while. We just never called it by that name.

It began attracting a lot more attention in the media through celebrities validating its benefits.

I mean if **Timothée Chalamet** is seen lunching with *Seinfeld* and *Curb Your Enthusiasm* creator **Larry David**, of all people, you think someone's going to notice—and think it is very cool?

Or what about the one and only **Lady Gaga** singing alongside **Tony Bennett**, who's been a recording star for more than sixty years?

And there has been no more famous symbol of intergenerational bonding than the one and only **Betty White**.

Under normal circumstances, when would a **Millennial** or **Gen Zer** (or even **Gen Xer** for that matter) be aware of a ninety-something-year-old actor? I could think of a whole lot of seventy-year-old actors today whose names would draw blank stares from younger generations.

Not Betty White, though. She had an extraordinary ability to relate to people of any age. Why? She just was herself. She didn't try to be hip, and in doing so, she was cooler than most Hollywood stars sixty years her junior! How many of those younger stars could move millions of fans to message NBC that they should host *Saturday Night Live* as Betty White did at eighty-eight, the oldest person ever to host the show?

If they were to build a monument to intergenerational bonding, they should sculpt it in the image of Betty White.

I have my own version of ***Intergenerational Bonding***. It is tied directly to what I see as its natural partner—***Mutual Mentoring***. I love the Fireside Chats and conversations about life I have at ***FIT***. It gives me a great opportunity to act as both teacher and student. *I Teach Them Business, They Teach Me Life!*

In those groups, I stress that the differences separating generations, which we are too quick to accept as inevitable, will become irrelevant, as the value of ***Intergenerational Bonding*** becomes more apparent and commonplace.

There's another term I've coined for bridging that age gap—***Generation Splicing***. That denotes fusing together diverse groups for mutual improvement and unified purpose.

Intergenerational Bonding has been embraced for many years by the medical profession as a way for the aging population to cope with loneliness, depression, and even physical maladies, such as heart problems and various diseases common to older generations.

The differences separating generations, which we are too quick to accept as inevitable, will become irrelevant, as the value of *Intergenerational Bonding* becomes more apparent and commonplace.

THE GENERATION GAP

The expression commonly used when **Baby Boomers** were the **Gen Z** of their era—the younger generation—was *The Generation Gap*.

A big deal was made at the time about the many differences that separated *Teenagers* and *Twentysomethings* from their parents and grandparents.

There were multiple flashpoints that reinforced the generational rift—drugs, war, politics, music, even physical appearance.

Different eras are defined by different standards of behavior, different values, even different language. It can be hard to relate to "the other" if you don't have the **Patience** and make an effort to find common ground, at least for the sake of a conversation. You never know what may come of it that is a revelation worth filing away in your head for future use.

If you were to listen in on the conversation of two people who are thirty or more years apart in age, there's a good chance that either of the people having the conversation won't relate to some of the words and expressions coming out of the other person's mouth.

For example, as part of my monthly **MAB** meetings, our group explores and comments on what's in vogue and what's not. Some of us in the older group learned that the word "cheugy" refers to what **Gen Zers** think is old-fashioned about **Millennials**. That's a good reminder that "old" is totally relative. A person of twenty-seven is "old" to a nineteen-year-old.

We went around the room with everyone giving examples of what they think is cheugy. It was a good exercise in intergenerational bonding (even if you think it was cheugy to do it).

Not only language but lifestyles in general vary from one generation to the next. **Millennials** are not nearly as enamored of owning their own home as their parents were at a comparable point in their lives.

The same can be said about how **Millennials** feel about owning a car. They don't consider it essential but a bigger expense than they want to take on.

That in turn leads to **Millennials** favoring the convenience of mixed-use living, where shelter, shopping, recreation, culture, and transportation are all within walking distance of each other.

Who is building all those mixed-use hubs? **Gen X** and **Baby Boomer** developers, that's who. Even that symbiotic relationship can be looked at as **Intergenerational Bonding**: one generation (the landlord) is enabling another generation (the tenant) to indulge their lifestyle choices.

That evolution of trends in living preferences is a legitimate mutual benefit. It helps the developer for obvious reasons, and it supports **Millennials** with quality of life choices that are more to their liking and reflect their values.

There are pockets of the country where different generations are living side by side in the same community, including college campuses that incorporate high-end housing for **Baby Boomers**.

There are other lessons I bring to the Fireside Chats at **FIT**. They are not theoretical. I don't believe in that BS. I'm like one of those celebrities who will not promote or endorse a product unless they actually use it and swear by it. Never underestimate the importance of being authentic.

DON'T LET LOGIC FOOL YOU

I offer only the advice I know works because it's worked for me in real life. I'm not much interested in "what-ifs" or simulations. That's not real life. It's fantasy land. I like Disney World as much as the next person but not when it comes to how I live my life or run my business.

One of my biggest lessons is to **not confuse issues with logic**. By that I mean don't assume that every successful strategy needs to sound logical. Not everything you'll come across in your career or life responds predictably to what we consider logical.

If something sounds crazy to you or not plausible, that doesn't mean it won't work or isn't the right thing to do. Some of my biggest wins came from going against the grain or challenging conventional wisdom. There are a lot of billionaires out there whose pronouncements and behavior can be called irrational. It hasn't held them back. They learned long ago that if you follow the crowd all the time, you'll get lost in it instead of rising above it.

Finding a good mentor is imperative. The "good" part doesn't travel only one way. You have to be as good for the mentor as that person is effective for you. That's the mutual part of **Mutual Mentoring**.

The hardest part of mentoring, in fact, is finding the person who is best for you. They don't grow on trees or necessarily hang around social media. It's like going on a hunting expedition. You have to forage for them.

> **Mentoring is more than just passive *Listening*. It's being an *active* Listener.**

First, you need to know what you're looking for. It takes detective work, followed by salesmanship, to convince the right person you're eager to learn and that you can offer something that they in turn want to learn. You have to give, not just take.

I don't want to give the wrong impression here. I am not saying you walk up to your target mentor and blurt out, "Can you mentor me?" It takes a bit more finesse than that.

I want to mentor someone who is obsessed with getting ahead. Do you project that? If you say you can learn a lot from someone, it flatters them, of course, but then you also have to show why you want to be *Mentored*. *Mentoring* is more than just passive *Listening*. It's being an active *Listener*. Weaponize your *Listening*! Again, that also plays into the mutual part.

Your ideal coach is out there somewhere. A lot of them will mentor you for a relatively brief period, and when you graduate or move to a new job, that *Mentorship* is over. You might get a season's greetings card from them after that, or you might not. They might check in with you to see how you're doing later on, or they might not. They might return your call or not.

MENTORING FOR LIFE

I don't work that way. If I'm going to commit to taking on someone as their *Mentor*, it is for life, not a semester or a year or as long as they work for me. I believe in *Mentoring* people for life.

I *Mentor* them about life as well as business. The two are inseparable. No matter which part of their life we're talking about, they are the same person. And I *Mentor* them for virtually the rest of their life. In my mind, *Mentoring* never ends. It's a lifelong contract. If it's ever broken, it's not because I broke it. If your work isn't your life and your life isn't your work, like I said in the first few pages, this book is not for you. I don't deal in *Timidity*. It gets you nowhere. It makes you less than you can be.

One of my sports heroes is **Duke University** men's basketball coach **Mike Krzyzewski** (a.k.a. **Coach K.**). Decades after he started his career, this guy still talks to former players he mentored decades ago. It's a matter of personal pride for him, but it's more than that. It's a matter of personal responsibility. He feels committed to them for life!

I'm with Coach K. One of the ways I evaluate the best candidates for **Mentorship** is whether they are only interested in "one and done" or are in it for the long haul.

There are those I have **Mentored** in my career—going back even thirty and more years—where the **Mentoring** never has stopped. It continues to this day. I don't mentor just for now or for their current job or situation. **I Mentor for life.** I firmly believe that's the only way it should work. More than that, for me, that is the only way I *will* work.

The people I am most interested in working with are those who assertively pursue **Mentorship**.

Also good to remember is that no matter how talented you might be at what you do, getting the job that best takes advantage of those skills is not a slam dunk. You need to work on cultivating connections that come through for you and are not just idle talk.

Anybody can talk. There are a lot of slick, fast talkers out there. I've seen them all. I've heard their patter. I'm not impressed.

It's authentic, quality people who will keep their word and act on it to help you. That's how you get ahead. That's how you work yourself into the position you covet.

As **FIT** Dean **Brooke Carlson** added at one of our Fireside Chats, "When you go into **Mutual Mentoring**, you must know exactly what you want, be clear about it, and it can't just be about you." I couldn't agree more with her words of wisdom.

I greatly value and respect the working relationship I have with Brooke Carlson and *FIT*. She really understands *Tribal Knowledge*. I am not sure I would have built the strong relationships I have with *FIT* grad students if she wasn't involved. That's especially true with the graduate students we *Mentor* since some of them also have jobs or run their own businesses.

To gain the trust of others, it also helps that Dean Carlson and I are empathetic in understanding the students' challenges. Those may be academic or about deciding on a career, which is the same as figuring out where you want your life to take you.

Brooke Carlson

By the way, do you take time every day—five minutes—to think that through? I believe the way to get ahead and stay there is to plan ahead. I may be more extreme and detailed than most that way—I can tell you what I'm going to do and where I'll be a year from today. So far it's gotten me where I want to go.

Whether or not you're *Mentoring* someone, exercising *Empathy* in daily life is an essential part of getting a life. I would not expect a roomful of ambitious graduate students to respond very well to me were I to pose at a podium and speechify as if I were giving a keynote at a business conference or a financial report at an annual shareholders meeting.

LET'S HAVE A CONVERSATION

I go the opposite direction. I sit down in Fireside Chats that Brooke has created for the students, and I converse with them instead of talking at them. That's how you connect with anybody you want to influence and whose attention you want to hold. Our Fireside Chats can last up to ninety minutes.

They're not paying me to do it. I'm paying them to do it! "Bob's not just giving us his money," said Dean Carlson. "He's giving us his time."

Even if I was being paid, the money wouldn't make me feel any more gratified than I do when I receive a note like the one *FIT* President Dr. Joyce Brown sent me.

Bob and Dr. Joyce Brown

"You have made quite an impact on the lives of our graduate students, and your ongoing support signifies your deep commitment to FIT and to our many multi-talented students. By all accounts, we are living through a period of unprecedented challenge. The steadfastness of your friendship and support is key to our continued success, and it is very gratifying."

There is no price you can put on that kind of feedback.

There are situations where *Mentorships* can happen organically. A teacher and a supervisor at your place of work are obvious examples of how that can work to your advantage since they are in proximity on a regular basis, and there already is continual interaction with them. Over time you build relationships, and the person starts mentoring you as a logical extension of that bonding.

Remember, too, that you can make connections that may not necessarily become *Mentorships*. Relationships can take other forms that are valuable in their own right.

As a CEO, I wasn't typical in a lot of ways. I pride myself on being a creative disruptor. I don't do it just to make mischief. I do it to shake things up when they need to be shaken. I do it to get people to see a different perspective that isn't obvious to everyone. I go with my gut because I trust it. I trust it because it's worked pretty well for me over the years. I'd be an idiot to ignore my instincts that have made a lot of people a lot of money.

One of my idiosyncrasies—a word conventional or boring CEOs might use to describe my style—is that I genuinely take a personal interest not just in the senior associates I have direct contact with. I engage with entry-level employees as well.

A REAL GO-GETTER

During one of our group dinners for *rue21* district managers at a Sheraton Hotel in Pittsburgh, I was told that one of our Teen Board members—fifteen-year-old *Meredith Michalojko* (a.k.a. *Meredith Michal*)—was on the premises and asking to come in to sit by me during dinner. Meredith also worked at *rue21*, and at the same time, she was pursuing modeling and acting. A real go-getter! My kind of mentee.

First off, I couldn't imagine what she was doing in the hotel, but no matter. Someone else in my position might think she was out of line or remarkably presumptuous to crash our dinner.

My reaction was the opposite. I was majorly impressed by how gutsy this young woman showed herself to be. I thought it was great of her to ask to come in and hang out with us.

Why would I turn her away if she was that hungry not only to learn our business but also to want to learn it directly from the CEO's point of view? I welcomed her in, and Meredith sat on her knees next to our table the rest of the dinner, soaking it all in.

I love that high level of self-motivation. It supports one of my core principles of personal achievement—***do whatever it takes***!

Right now Meredith is a producer in California. I never doubted she'll prove successful in almost anything she sets her strong-willed mind to do.

SAY NO TO BEING A KNOW-IT-ALL

As arrogant and aggressive as I was known by some to be, I knew enough to balance that cockiness with well-placed humility.

The advice I pass along is to be careful not to act like you have all the answers. Sometimes people will act as if "You don't need to tell me that. I know exactly what to do." I always believed that people above me were a lot more knowledgeable than me. When I was in my thirties, I knew full well that I was a beginner and certainly didn't have all the answers.

The same holds true when searching for a *Mentor*. It's not productive to act like you know more than the person you're trying to learn from. Someone can have great vision and creativity yet still have a hard time taking it to fruition. You need the experience of the *Boomer*, and you need to believe it, not just go through the motions. Showing the *Boomer* who might be *Mentoring* you that you respect their experience and care about what they have to say is part of *Reverse Mentoring*.

It helps to learn about the potential **Mentor** as much as you can. Here's a good trick I learned in business that can be adapted to this goal. People will talk a lot when you meet them. Some of it could be personal chitchat along with business banter.

Make a note of what they said that was meaningful. It might be a random thought. Or an idea about a project or new product. Or it might be about their kids. The next time you see them, even if it's weeks later, bring up something they said during the prior meeting.

In my case I sometimes would repeat even a couple of months later what they said. You're validating their thoughts. It's a way of selling yourself as engaged, focused, goal-oriented, and part of the team.

That technique worked for me in board meetings, which can become contentious and political. I had to be like a symphony conductor to walk out of those meetings with the board fully behind what I wanted to do. But I couldn't stand there and act as if "This is what we're doing. My mind is made up." That's an invitation to dissent and second-guessing—and having your initiative voted down.

Instead, if my plan was to open 100–125 stores, I would say, "Do you think 75 stores is too aggressive?" Board members might shoot back, "No, let's go for 100." Some might call that kind of ploy sandbagging. I call it smart negotiating based on understanding human nature.

Similarly, I am not going to stand up at a meeting with graduate students and bloviate, "This is why you should learn from me and why I made a lot of money."

No. The objective is to convince them "This is what I can do for you."

That's also how you should sell yourself to a future **Mentor**. "What's in it for me?" never goes out of fashion. Whether it's intergenerational bonding or selling dresses, every relationship is transactional in that sense.

Who's *your* **Mentor**?

TAKE A TRIP TO THE OTHER SIDE

Macon Brock

Don't make the mistake of assuming how a person you don't know thinks or acts based on their appearance or their age. It's foolish to stereotype people from afar just because they are from a different generation than you or because you can't relate to their fashion style.

An excellent example of how an open-minded attitude can produce positive results is my late friend *Macon Brock*, who was on my board of directors at *rue21*. Macon was the founder and former CEO and Chairman of *Dollar Tree*, a pioneer in discount merchandising.

✎ In a discussion I had with him about succession, Macon told me how he decided who the next-generation CEO would be to take over from him. There was one candidate on the short list about whom Macon had some mixed feelings. This potential CEO was different from Macon in his thinking, which concerned the founder. He understandably wanted the person he selected to not only preserve his *Legacy* but also build on it for future growth.

※ In the end, though, Macon went with what his instinct told him, which was that this was the best person to lead Dollar Tree as the next-generation CEO. Macon accepted that his successor didn't have to think or behave exactly like him if he clearly was the most qualified candidate in every other way. And he was. Whatever minor reservations Macon might have had became the smartest business decision. How smart was it? In his years running the company, Dollar Tree CEO Bob Sasser tripled the number of Dollar Tree stores.

※ It's good to be emotional in embracing your work, but you can't let negative emotions get in the way of making the right decision. As Macon Brock did, you need to keep an *Open Mind* about people and ideas that may not feel right at first.

※ Expanding your consciousness that way can help you in every part of your life. But only if you make an *Honest*, serious effort to apply what you learn from the other person.

※ Instead of avoiding the "other"—someone not to your liking, for instance—make it your business to embrace the "other." Bond with them, value their *Mentorship*, and generously offer your *Mentorship* to them. It may not be easy to do that at first, but it may help you keep in mind how well that realization worked for Macon Brock and Dollar Tree.

GET A VISION

TO MOVE FORWARD in achieving your goals, the best advice I can give is to go backward. That's not nearly as illogical as it sounds. When we are traveling somewhere, with or without GPS, don't we need an address in our possession to arrive at the destination?

In our work life and in our homelife, that destination takes the form of a ***Vision***. Not to have a ***Vision*** of where you want to go in life is to proceed blind. Even those who are ***Vision***-impaired know where they're going. The difference is that their ***Vision*** is virtual rather than literal.

Let's start with ***Listening***, which we've already covered, but it is relevant here too. Why? Think of ***Vision***—and how to use it to your advantage—as ***Listening*** with your eyes. When you ***Listen*** well to others—whether with your ears or eyes—you're able to develop critical thinking to help put together the pieces of the puzzle that are part of every decision you make. And every decision you make leads you to one of three places—closer to your goals, or further away, or neither, just stuck in place.

I had to get good at *Listening* when I became a CEO at the age of thirty-six. It's a key skill in business and in life. First, you have to *Listen* carefully to your customers. Many people don't do that well. Second, *Listen* to your bosses—*Listen* hard to what they say and evaluate that. Third, *Listen* intently to the people around you, whether family or colleagues.

If you aren't trusting what you hear, you need to be able to dig into why. *(For more on Listening, see Chapter 5: It's All about PECPL.)*

Your *Vision* is the essential foundation of building for the future. Remember, the future may be distant from the past, but they are connected. Embracing the future with the past is important.

Just as your hearing must be unobstructed to understand what is being said, your *Vision* also is influenced by your past. The *Vision* must be clear, focused, and cannot be too distracted.

Motivational Mentor Bill Wooditch, on whose *The Unstoppables* podcast I have been a guest, warns about how distractions can cloud your *Vision*. Bill and I hit it off immediately because we discovered that we had a lot in common in our philosophy on leadership.

> **Your *Vision* is the essential foundation of building for the future.**

THE ATTRACTION OF DISTRACTION

"Every day you encounter distractions," Wooditch says, that threaten to sidetrack you from your goals. "It's the salesperson," he says, as an example, "who, instead of making cold calls, creates files, rearranges the office space daily, [and] takes an hour in the break room before, during, and after lunch." Is that you? I hope not. If it is, admit it and fix it.

How do you get a *Vision*? First and foremost, it must be rooted in reality. I'm not saying it shouldn't be *Ambitious* and *Aspirational*. It absolutely should! I'm also not saying you should *Stay in Your Lane*, four words that I despise as not *realistic*, and which I address further in *chapter 5*.

By staying rooted in reality, I mean *acting* on your *Vision*. In the business world, there are two types of people. Those who talk and talk and talk and those who talk and execute, execute, execute.

I've learned that there are a lot of people who talk a good game. Maybe more of those people than the real deals—those who see their *Vision* through to fruition, whether or not they talk a good game.

Being slick and smooth on the outside is not a sign of accomplishment, or of smarts, or of marketable talent. It's a charm offensive that may fool some people, but I'm not one of those people. I size up people quickly. I learned to do that on the job. It's a survival technique. I don't intend to be easily fooled by the charmers. It used to bother me when I couldn't understand somebody right away. I got rid of that limitation. To me, oozing charm is superficial; it's icing on the cake. I want to be impressed initially by what the person is made of—by the quality of the ingredients that were used to bake the cake.

Why care about getting a *Vision*?

Everybody can make something of themselves that is better than what they think they are—or at least try to do something that seems out of reach, like a dream.

The point is that getting a *Vision* is how you make something of yourself. Don't just sit still and try to figure out how to get by as if that's enough and the rest doesn't really matter.

WHAT WILL YOU BE KNOWN FOR?

There's no purpose to that. If anything, you should feel fortunate and humble about the *Opportunities* available to you. That's why this book is not for everybody. *It's certainly not for the timid.* I don't care if someone wants to be the best salesperson or best designer or best doctor. You want to be known for *something*, don't you? *(Learn more about this in Chapter 13: Get a Legacy.)*

Bob and Nammy Patel

Bob and Steve Forbes

Speaking of exceptional people who practice medicine, meet **Dr. Namrata "Nammy" Patel**. When I met Nammy at a special gathering of Forbes Books authors hosted by **Forbes Media** CEO **Steve Forbes** and Forbes Books CEO Adam Witty, I could tell right away she is special—and a great role model for this book's **Get a Life** message.

A native of India, her family moved to America when Nammy was five years old. Being a foreigner in unfamiliar surroundings forced her to seek **Mentors** to help her find the right career path.

As a child, she was instilled with the values of conserving, recycling, and respecting the environment. After putting herself through the University of Southern California School of Dentistry, she had a **Vision** of a "green" dental practice that combined exceptional patient care with minimizing environmental impact.

The result of her **Vision** is **Green Dentistry**, the practice she founded in 2015 that was the first of its kind in San Francisco. Within its first nine months of existence, **Green Dentistry** was a million-dollar practice but not without Nammy putting in sixteen-hour days. In subsequent years her practice grew 25 to 30 percent every year.

"Things don't always go exactly as we anticipate," says Nammy, "but it's our job to figure how to best maneuver and fix the situation. I was committed and had the passion and drive. I would do whatever it took to get my practice to another level."

Nammy's *Vision* is summed up by a quote of hers that could be a motto for anyone who is obsessed with performing at the very highest levels of whatever is their *Vision*: "I'm not interested in being ordinary. I'm interested in being extraordinary."

She adds, "It's just not in my DNA to do something subpar. My focus has always been on giving back, purpose, and passion. In this day and age, my [mission] is all about maintaining quality and exchange of energy. I'm always conscious about what I can do to make it better, faster, and easier on my patients. I compartmentalize and focus on being fully present on my patient's needs."

SEEKING GREATER ACCOMPLISHMENTS

Dr. Patel advises entrepreneurs to solve a unique problem and, like her, to focus on service. "Trust yourself about the relationship and journey," she advises. "Founding a business is an immense opportunity for learning and personal growth. We all want to be rewarded, but we also want to accomplish things that are greater than us—outside of who we are and what we do."

My *Vision* to run an apparel retail chain was formed years ago in my positions at major merchants such as Jordan Marsh, Casual Corner, *rue21*, and even in my first gig after college, at A&S. Almost as soon as I started at A&S, I had a *Vision*. It was that, within a dozen years, I was going to be CEO of a major retail corporation. Admittedly, it took me a while to reach that conclusion, a full week.

I wanted to exercise my creative instincts to build an innovative retail operation, which is what happened with *rue21*. Setting my mind to something in a dream always comes true. That was how I harnessed the power of *Vision* to create a leading innovator in value-priced, fast-fashion retailing.

I wasn't motivated purely by financial gain but because it's what I enjoyed doing, and I was confident it would succeed. I knew I could build a business, but I had no idea of the rewards it would bring years later. I didn't know at first that we'd grow *rue21* to 1,200 stores. I didn't know we'd sell *rue21* for $1 billion-plus. Those were the unseen results of my hard work, not my single-minded goals. There's a difference.

Sure, I knew what I wanted, but I didn't know I'd get everyone sitting there to believe in me.

That's one of the tests you face when other people are affected by your *Vision*. Beyond getting a *Vision*, you need to get others to trust your *Vision* if their livelihoods also depend on your *Vision* coming to fruition.

Beyond getting a *Vision*, you need to get others to trust your *Vision* if their livelihoods also depend on your *Vision* coming to fruition.

MARKETING YOUR VISION

Even when you are wholly confident that your *Vision* will take hold, being *Visionary* in that sense means you have to be careful how you describe it to people so you don't scare them away.

With any *Vision* I've had, I was obsessed with whatever I wanted to happen. As said elsewhere in this book, my strong belief is that someone who is not obsessed does not really want to attain what they claim is their *Vision*. It means taking a risk, which is the only way anyone can achieve great things they want for themselves.

You must have a zest for life to have a *Vision* of who you want to be and what you want to do. It means looking ahead by living outside the moment. At the same time, it means staying present with the job at hand by staying within the moment. Hey, nobody said becoming successful and living your dream would be—or should be—easy. To make matters more interesting, it's not only about what you know you want. It helps to not shut the door on what you didn't realize you want. An open mind will open opportunities you didn't recognize at first.

Life is a series of contradictions, of conflicts, of contrasts and opposites. Don't fight them. Use them. Let circumstances guide you, and at the same time, make the circumstances work for you.

A *Vision* is constantly evolving. It is the concept of reinvention. You can create things in your mind that turn into reality. I still get the itch on doing certain things in the retail sector even though I'm not running a retail organization. I think about how much fun it would be to strategize and grow the business.

After *rue21*, my head was spinning with possibilities, anchored by a master *Vision* of how I wanted the next chapter in my life to play out.

I knew I didn't want to sit around and just think about what I *could* be doing. I wanted to get out and do it.

By the way, I get a lot of ideas when I run on the treadmill. Nothing's better for getting my mind excited than pushing my body to its limits. Sometimes I'll write the ideas down as soon as I get off so they don't run away from me after I'm finished running.

HAVE IT YOUR WAY

Like I've said, when I put my mind to something, it usually takes root and happens. It's not magic. I think hard about it, and when necessary I force the issue by getting other people to see things my way.

When I was interviewed by *Human Resource Executive* magazine, I said, "*Millennials* tell me, 'Don't stop pushing yourself because you don't stop pushing us.'" And I do push them—I tell them if they want to get ahead, they need to speak up and stand up for what they believe in.

When **Rusty Shelton**, host of podcast *Authority Marketing*, interviewed me, he agreed, noting, "People who want it and push for it accelerate their careers like nobody else."

I've been a **Disruptor** all my life because I stand up for what I believe in. Being that way is why I wasn't satisfied by only creating the **Millennial Baby Boomer**® brand. I had it registered as proprietary intellectual property in my name, as its owner, with the U.S. Patent and Trademark Office.

How you lead your life brings you to your future. In my case, even years after leaving *rue21*, I am constantly at work, finding ways to seize opportunities, such as authoring two books, forming a **Millennial Advisory Board** that meets monthly, serving on the Board of Directors of four-hundred-plus-store retail chain **Ollie's Bargain Outlet**, becoming active on social media, and investing a sizable portion of time and financial support in my affiliation with **FIT**.

That's not to say that, after the *rue21* years, I had a detailed game plan immediately. I simply knew that total reinvention is important to keep yourself mentally active and a vital part of society. If I'm telling young people to do that, I have to live my own advice and do it as well.

I'm not all that different from you or from other people; I'm a regular person. It's what you challenge yourself to do that separates the *Doers* from the *Don'ters*. Which one are you? Which one do you want to be?

Forming a *Vision* in my mind and then mapping out how it would surface in the real world is how I created my multilayered alliance with *FIT*. It grew out of my *Passion* to make a difference in the lives of others, especially those in whom I see genuine passion and a clear *Vision* of what they want to do and who they want to become. I honestly can say, even with all I'm proud of accomplishing at *rue21* and elsewhere before that, I've never felt more fulfillment than I do working with students, faculty, and administrators at *FIT*. Whatever monetary gifts I give to them are outweighed by the gift I get in return by being welcomed into the inner circle of a great institution of higher learning.

ROOTED IN REALITY

An important part of the *Vision* I formed with *FIT* is to impart wisdom and inspire others like me to not only donate monetarily but also share their lifetime of wisdom. Like they say, *Time Is Money*, so spending a generous amount of time to sit with *FIT* students pays dividends not only for them but for the faculty as well. It supports their efforts and instills in students a valuable view of what the real world of fashion design and management is like. In order for them to form strong *Visions* for their future, it's important that they don't have any illusions about the industry. That's one way I help their *Visions* stay rooted in reality.

How my *FIT Vision* materialized also is a good lesson in *Patience*. It's not as if I just snapped my fingers and it was a done deal. It took more than two years from concept to completion of the first phase of the several programs I sponsor in conjunction with *FIT* president Dr. Joyce Brown and other administrators at *FIT*. *(For more on Patience, see Chapter 5: It's All about PECPL.)*

After months of negotiating and refining what my contributions would entail, it was a very heady feeling of fulfillment that came over me when the *Vision* I had started describing in March 2020 to *FIT* was announced to the world with this October 2021 headline in fashion industry bible *Women's Wear Daily:* "*FIT Launches Bob Fisch Graduate Student Award Program.*"

As the article described, my role at *FIT* covers a lot of ground, with a focus on the central strategy of *Intergenerational Bonding*.

This quote from me in the article connects the dots of my *Vision*.

> *"I am delighted to present this gift to **FIT** to help nurture the careers of future leaders in the retail space. As the leading college of its kind in America, **FIT** serves as a major talent pipeline, which I hope to enrich through the establishment of this new program. I'm a firm believer in the benefits of **Intergenerational Bonding** and **Mutual Mentoring** as there is much I can learn from the students' questions and curiosity, just as they can learn from my answers and experience. I teach them business ... They teach me life."*

EVERYBODY WINS

The best practices I impart to the graduate students are being incorporated as well into the school's curriculum. All of these initiatives contribute to my *FIT Vision* of supporting its flagship graduate program, helping boost the school's recruitment and retention of top students, adding a unique point of differentiation, elevating the students' learning experience, and contributing to their ongoing career development.

In short, my role at *FIT* is to give back in a multitude of ways and motivate other board members and alumni to do the same. It's building on something where the *Vision* is clear to see so other people can easily follow. My message to them is that it's not a chore to *Give Back* but a blessing. Rather than treat it like a big deal, I see it as a natural impulse we all should have to be purposeful in thinking about how to give back.

As a basketball fan, I like to point to the *Vision* that helped make the late *Kobe Bryant* of the *Los Angeles Lakers* one of the greatest to play the game.

As an eighteen-year-old, he was drafted by the National Basketball Association directly out of high school. From the get-go, he exuded *Discipline*, *Commitment*, *Confidence*, *Trust*, *Loyalty*, and a *Maturity* way beyond his years.

He even set his sights at that tender age of one day being compared with the one and only *Michael Jordan*. That was his lifelong *Vision*.

Kobe also had a *Vision* that motivated his game performances. "The competitive side of me feels we can win every game we play. What I've learned is to always keep going. Learn to love the process."

Said his teammate *Pau Gasol*, "Kobe knew to be the best, you needed a different approach from everyone else."

THE VALUE OF DIFFERENT

I fully relate to that mindset because I was looked at in my industry as a maverick who did not feel the need to follow conventional wisdom. I, too, had a different approach, and I'd do it the same way again. If you want to be like everybody else, you'll blend into the faceless crowd. In his twenty-year career, Kobe elevated himself above everyone else and not just when making an emphatic slam dunk but every minute of every game.

"If you do the work, dreams come true," he said. "Get up early and work hard. Stay up late and work hard. If you're too tired, push yourself, do it anyway. I wanted to be one of the best. Anything outside that lane, I didn't have time for."

Pursuing a *Vision* has risks. Anything worthwhile does, of course. Bill Wooditch has excellent advice about how to manage your *Vision*'s risks to give it the best chance of being fulfilled.

"Before you take a risk, know your worst case. Write it down. Then start to do those things to manage that worst case while building towards your upside. You first have to know what winning is, what it means, what it looks like, what it feels like. Write that down. So you have the worst case, and you have the best case. How do you get there?"

Wooditch continues, "Then take those small steps toward that best possible outcome. Once you've figured out what works, get out your journal and make detailed notes. Write down everything that brought you closer to a successful outcome. As you build your profile, you will find an armory of successful strategies and tactics to draw from as you surge toward your next victory. The winner does not allow events outside their control to define their self-worth—failure doesn't dominate their thoughts; learning how to win does."

Bill and I are kindred spirits in many ways. If you fear that the steps he lays out for converting a *Vision* into a win is intimidating, that's okay. Sometimes you have to work hard to get the *Vision* to work. The harder you work at it, the more it can not only happen as you saw it but also expand beyond what you envisioned.

How do you go about getting a *Vision*?

WHAT'S THE GOOD WORD?

There's a simple way to get your mind motivated to figure it out. Simply put, to get a *Vision*, first get a *Word*.

Think of them as buzzwords. They are important because eventually they turn into fully formed ideas, which in turn become a *Vision*. That's why words can be quite powerful if you build on them and use them to sharpen and to shape your *Vision*.

I have key words I use when I'm talking to *FIT* students or mentoring anybody else. One of those is *Feisty*. That's how I think of myself. That's what I stand for. Feisty is my being consumed, pushing limits, teaching students not to hold back.

When I was a guest on *Lucinda Kay*'s *Speaking Freely* podcast, she introduced me by saying, "He was a *Badass* CEO." I liked that. *Badass* is a colorful word that speaks volumes.

I think of *Badass* in the same spirit as *Disruptor*—both are words that used to carry a negative connotation but now are considered high compliments. Being a *Badass* now means you care about what you do and take it seriously and, as a result, are very good at what you do.

Being a **Badass** means you inspire others to follow you toward success. There are some memorable quotes about that last word that I think are worth passing along here.

In our **Millennial Advisory Board**, at the start of each year, I frame a single word as our overall theme for the year. For example, 2022's word was **Fearless**, and in 2021 it was **Savage** (which could be seen as in the same family as **Badass**). You might want to do the same as one of your New Year's resolutions when the next January 1 rolls around.

I also ask **MAB** members to select their own word that they will live by for the entire year as a personal motivating prompt.

To help you get started and to give you the flavor of what kinds of words work for other people, here's a sampling of which words have been put to good use by my **MAB** members:

Ageless	*Focus*
Ambitious	*Resilience*
Appreciation	*Tenacity*
Energy	*Truth*

I've talked about another all-important word that is mandatory for leading a quality life. See if you can identify that key word in this quote from actor and entrepreneur **Ryan Reynolds**: "**Empathy** has gotten me so much farther in not only my life, but in my career." You didn't have to read very far to find it, did you?

What about you? What is the one word you want to live by to get you farther in your life and your career, and what are you going to do to make that word work for you and your **Vision**?

Ready? Then get set and get a **Word**, get a **Vision**, and get going.

RULES OF REINVENTION

VISION QUEST

🐟 A *Vision* is cousin to a *Calling*. A *Calling* comes to you as a *Passion* to do something productive and gratifying with your life. Creating a specific *Vision* to achieve that is how you turn your *Calling* into a *Legacy*.

🐟 Develop *Critical Thinking* to keep moving toward your *Vision*. Each decision you make along the way has one of three outcomes: it will help you progress, regress, or stagnate. Choose wisely.

🐟 Stay *Focused*! Like droplets of rain on eyeglasses, distractions blur your *Vision*.

🐟 Be a *Doer*, not a *Don'ter*. Talk is cheap. Taking *Action* is the gold standard of achieving your *Vision*.

🐟 Aim for being *Extraordinary*. Reach above and beyond to exceed your own expectations.

🐟 Don't avoid *Risks*. Embrace them.

🐟 Stay open to *Opportunities* you don't think are in your wheelhouse. You might surprise yourself with how well you adapt to them. A *Vision* is constantly evolving.

🐟 Speak up and *Stand Up* for your *Beliefs* and *Goals*.

🐟 To fulfill your *Vision*, the most important time to push harder is when you are *too tired* to push harder.

🐟 Get a single *Word* that keeps you moving *Obsessively* toward your *Vision*. If you find yourself drifting off course, that *Word* is your mantra that resets your compass to true north.

IT'S ALL ABOUT PECPL

Patience
Empathy
Curiosity
Passion
Listening

IF YOU ARRANGE the first letter of each of these human qualities into an acronym—PECPL—it almost looks like it says PEOPLE, doesn't it? I don't think that's a coincidence. Patience. Empathy. Curiosity. **PECPLE** Passion. Listening. Those are core values that people should be all about, aren't they? It doesn't matter who we are, what we do, who we know. We all are all the better if we work hard at each of those talents.

Those five virtues are intertwined. It's hard, if not impossible, to separate them. They work together. They are like a tight-knit team of all-stars. When they are smoothly operating, in sync with each other and with the world out there, they are like superpowers.

Everything you do in life and business is influenced by your Personal Values, so it's important you know what they are and that you are proud of them.

They also are the building blocks of Tribal Knowledge, one of the core themes of this book.

In addition to the five character traits amplified in this chapter, other Personal Values to strive for, and which pop up in this book, include Authenticity, Caring, Consistency, Honesty, Humility, Kindness, Respect, Responsibility, and Giving Back.

The one-word shorthand that reflects the sum of Personal Values is Integrity.

A man I greatly admire is ***Jerry Chazen***. When the former CEO of legendary fashion brand ***Liz Claiborne*** died in February 2022, the headline in *Women's Wear Daily* said it all, calling him "A Man of Integrity." A former CEO of Bloomingdale's was quoted as saying, "Jerry was always honorable. He was a man of his word [who] epitomized that you can do business with great Integrity."

Now let's take a closer look at PECPL.

PECPL

PATIENCE

It's easy to equate *Patience* with leaning back and taking it easy. That's so wrong!

We didn't build *rue21* to 1,200 stores by leaning back or twiddling our thumbs, waiting for something to happen. That steady growth required *Patience*. We first had to put ourselves through chapter 11 reorganization and wait for that process to play out. We weren't forced into declaring bankruptcy. We chose to go that route. That carefully devised strategy took a lot of *Patience*, both to figure it out and then to wait it out. And you know what? It worked as well as I envisioned it.

What that example tells you, and what learning the value of *Patience* teaches you, is that it is okay to dream big, as influencer *Gary "Vee" Vaynerchuk* likes to say, but as I like to say, you need to be realistic. Practicality of life is what I am all about.

Patience is not merely about the passage of time. It's about self-discipline and having a *Vision*. *Patience* is not about waiting for things to happen. It's about making things happen. It's about planning. You know what happens when you run too fast without a plan. You trip. You stumble. You hurt yourself. In your haste you slow yourself down, if not lose ground instead of making ground.

> *Patience* is not about waiting for things to happen. It's about *making* things happen.

Being *Patient* pushes you to new levels and new horizons. It doesn't stop you from enjoying life.

Patience is also about working with people who you're not going to always agree with or even necessarily like. In those situations *Patience* is an ally that gives you an opportunity to show you are not going to be petty, which can result in self-sabotage if you're not careful or if you underestimate the influence or authority of the person you can't stomach.

As a manager or senior executive, *Patience* allows you to nurture talent on your team who may be rough around the edges or inexperienced or too eager to impress at the expense of others' emotional well-being.

Our modern world has given us another inarguable reason to practice *Patience*. Longevity!

Thanks to huge advances in healthcare, it's not inconceivable that many *Gen Zers* and *Millennials* can live to one hundred-plus. Living longer, where the age range we know as "middle age" keeps inching upward, brings with it the need to pace ourselves.

"*Patience* and *Perseverance* obviously go together," says Adam Witty of Forbes Books.

Bob and Adam Witty

"This is one of the challenges young people have today. Society says everything needs to be done immediately. Jeff Bezos has spoiled us, and the drive-through lines have spoiled us, and everything online has spoiled us, to where, hey, you need something and instantly you

have it. In a career things don't happen instantly. I've had in my career a number of people who were frightened and talented, and they leave early because they were impatient, and they didn't feel they were getting promoted fast enough.

*"**Patience** and **Perseverance** is when you discover your **Calling**—and most people don't. You can be **Patient** and **Persevere** towards it because you know how important it is to you. When you don't know your **Calling**, simply have a job, you're more likely to jump around for a couple thousand extra dollars or because the grass seems greener on the other side. Those people end up being less satisfied professionally because they're just chasing something. They don't have a **Calling** that is reinforcing a longer-term vision."*

Adam credits his patience with letting him *Persevere* through the inevitable periods of self-doubt and frustration when the arc of his business wasn't going the way he wanted: "There would have been a number of places on my journey where any logical person would have quit. And because I know my *Calling*, and because when you know your *Calling* you can have a vision for the future, you're able and willing to be patient." His patience definitely paid off because he has built a very strong business in ForbesBooks.

When I was at *Casual Corner*, I was confident that I could build a value-priced apparel retail business. Where I was proved wrong is that those stores only needed to be located in outlets. They also need to be in strip centers and value malls. By the time I was at *rue21*, I had learned from the past and adapted. I had to have *Patience* to process that lesson.

Sometimes it works the other way: if you are convinced you are right about a decision that others doubt or disagree with, you need *Patience* to get your point across. In due time you must say to yourself, it will happen, but first I must lay the foundation to get others on board.

When I hatched my idea to work with *FIT* as a mentor and donor, initially there was something lost in translation between my concept and the way it was received at the other end.

From the time we started talking about my endowment to the school and how I would *Mentor* the students until the time it was finalized took almost fifteen months. That resulted in some frustration, but I didn't walk away from the partnership that had started to evolve between me and the school. I remained steady in pushing the direction I had in mind so all stakeholders understood the game plan.

With the Miami Heat, I'm looking at a similar strategy. We've gone back and forth on what kind of *Mentoring* and scholarship opportunities I might be able to provide and to whom within the NBA franchise. I know it will take *Patience* for me to move the needle so that both they and I meet on common ground with clear mutual benefit.

In a post-pandemic culture, *Patience* is a more valuable commodity than ever. Why? Because you can't make up for the time you lost during the pandemic. It only will make you more miserable. It's time to move ahead, not backward.

If the pandemic prompted you to pursue a different career path or, more specifically, a different job, be patient. Do your research. Think twice before jumping. Like the old expression goes, and is no less true than it ever was, the grass is always greener on the other side. Until you get there. Make sure you know where you're headed. Don't overvalue it. Don't undervalue where you are, unless you're utterly miserable and hate going to work every day.

Sometimes it's okay *not* to have *Patience*.

I have no **Patience** for **Boomers** without the imagination to welcome what's new and exciting in the world.

I have no **Patience** for **Millennials** and **Gen Xers** who think their life is over by thirty if their career hasn't taken off yet.

The question to ask is, Why hasn't it taken off? Life isn't over in your thirties, but on the other hand, if you *wait* for good things to happen, you could be waiting a long time. Then it's too late. Make things happen around you!

EMPATHY

One of the most cited characteristics of Millennials, if you excuse my generalizing an entire generation, is their impressive capacity for **Empathy**. It's especially evident in their concern—their **Passion**—for global causes such as climate change, protecting the environment, food insecurity, health challenges in third-world countries, and so on.

There also is the need for **Empathy** between generations. That idea is at the heart of my **Millennial Baby Boomer®** brand. With so much focus on the Millennial generation, I felt that it was overdue to create a relatable bridge to more actively connect that generation with **Baby Boomers**. I call it **Generation Splicing**. It's all about how **Millennials** and **Baby Boomers** can bridge the generation gap, and that is all about **Empathy**.

You don't have to be the CEO or the owner of a company to demonstrate **Empathy** for the place where you work. It entails understanding the needs of your colleagues, of your managers, and most importantly, of your customers. As one of my **Millennial Advisory Board** members, **Brian Tunick**, put it during the pandemic, "Our entire country needs to be more empathetic and understand what everyone is going through out there." That always will hold true, pandemic or not.

Just as I advocate **Mutual Mentoring**, **Empathy** in the workplace is a two-way street. Management needs to give workers not only material resources but moral support too. It should educate workers about upper management's responsibilities, whether it reports to shareholders or to a private equity owner. The more a company's human resources appreciate the challenges, frustrations, and imperatives weighing on the C-suite, the more they'll grow individually and in sync with the corporate culture.

Besides, workers who appreciate what it is like to be in a company's senior ranks are the talent most likely to land there themselves. Management that doesn't show **Empathy** toward workers ends up with a serious morale problem. Workers who don't show **Empathy** toward management end up either flatlining in the same job indefinitely or out the door definitely.

On a one-to-one basis, showing your supervisor **Empathy** can be as simple as acting out the timeless business advice not to bring a problem to their office unless you also bring a solution. Otherwise, you're just pushing your problems onto their desk. If you're routinely expecting a supervisor to solve your issue when you walk in, after a while they're going to question your value to them and to the company.

Empathy is **Caring**. Part of **Empathy** at work is letting your bosses see you **Care** about more than your paycheck. Show them demonstrably that you have a personal investment in the performance of your department and the company as a whole. You can do that by *not* timidly staying in your lane. Instead, jump out of it when you can and volunteer to help in areas other than what your job description says.

Vulnerability and *Humility* are relatives of *Empathy*. People gravitate to those who are strong enough to allow their *Vulnerable* side to show through. The biggest myth about human nature, especially among men, is that it's the tough ones who never admit mistakes. Wrong!

It takes a lot more toughness to be secure enough to admit when you did something wrong. By not admitting weakness, you show weakness. By admitting weakness, you show strength. In its own way, that is the most powerful form of *Empathy*, to say "I know I don't know it all, so maybe I can learn something from you." Who doesn't love hearing that?

Seeing things from other people's perspectives is important for your success. People typically think about what they want and not how what they want is perceived by others. We all know people, including our closest friends, who don't always listen closely to what you are saying. They are texting when someone else is talking, or if they are really versatile, they are texting while eating with you. That's showing lack of *Respect*.

A different kind of *Empathy* was called into question during the pandemic, and as it subsided, people who became exceedingly comfortable working from their home office resisted returning to their normal places of work, which some hadn't occupied for up to two years.

In effect, home office workers lost *Empathy* for the physical space they had occupied before the pandemic. Can you have *Empathy* for an office? That depends whether you believe in feng shui or not. A lot of people do. For the record, that is defined as "a system of laws considered to govern spatial arrangement and orientation in relation to the flow of energy, and whose favorable or unfavorable effects are taken into account when siting and designing buildings."

One of the hallmarks of my management style was to treat people like a big family. I made it a point to be considerate of their lives. They would come to my office when they did something out of the ordinary and proudly tell me, "Look what I did!"

Another way I made **Empathy** part of our corporate culture was holding fun events like an *Alter Ego* party. It lets people learn about each other beyond the confines of their cubicle. When people appreciate each other's personal sides more, it helps them have more **Empathy** for each other.

When I learned that *Julie Fanning*, the manager of the health club I belong to, *Equinox Flatiron*, needed to find an apartment in a hurry, I reached out to offer help if she needed it. How many execs take their time to make somebody else successful, somebody who may not even work for them? How many people in life go out of their way to help a nonfamily member? What about you?

What percent of people take others under their wing and monitor their progress? I didn't do that with everybody because that would be impractical, but it was always on my mind to try to help wherever I could. Be selfless as a leader. If you worry about others being successful, you will be very successful.

Always show *Patience* and *Empathy*. I was fortunate to run businesses where I felt that way about wanting to help people.

When I left *rue21*, what was most important to me was that people knew I always showed *Patience* and *Empathy* and that while I was tough when it was right for the company, I was also fair, and people trusted me.

It's important to understand the difference between being *Empathetic* yet not taking things personally or in the wrong way. For instance, a stronger *Mentor* will make you a stronger leader by saying what you need to hear, not what you want to hear. That's where **Listening** enters the picture.

As stated in *Fisch Tales: The Making of a Millennial Baby Boomer*, the way I've been able to advance my position and my ideas over the years is to treat each person as someone of distinct value. I don't just call myself *Millennial Baby Boomer*®. I live it. My goal is to inspire separate generations to *Empathize* more fully with each other in a way that turns *Personal Values* into shared values.

PEC**PL**

LISTENING

One of the questions I always ask people I mentor is how hard they push to achieve what they can do? Also, do they *Listen?*

You don't want to stop yourself from going further by not *Listening* to people who can help you.

As I mentioned elsewhere in *Get a Life*, when the real estate director for *Casual Corner* said we shouldn't focus only on outlet centers, instead of thinking, "Here is an arrogant older guy," I thought maybe I can learn from him.

You have to go after what you believe and still keep an open mind. Think about what is the right thing to do and how to utilize that going forward. You think you have the answers, but you also need to know who to listen to.

Listening is not just hearing somebody talk. It's taking action based on what they say. People don't hear things well or don't want to. People like that don't listen because they are insecure or don't think others can help them.

Do young people *Listen* and *Learn* for the future? When running a business, it's not that you don't *Listen*, but you're an island sometimes. That's where weaponizing *Listening* is extremely important.

A stronger *Mentor* will make you a stronger leader by saying what you need to hear, not what you want to hear. Weaponizing *Listening* is more than merely saying, "I hear you." Are you receptive enough to act on what you are being advised? I learned that more as I matured in business because I was not good enough at it when I was younger.

During my time at Casual Corner, one December several employees asked me about their profit-sharing checks. I told them, "We didn't make a profit this year." Their tone-deaf reply was "What does that matter? I always get my check at the end of the year."

How do you make a difference of what you want to do in your life? *Listening* is being part of conversation and also hearing what others have to say. Those people didn't hear me; they chose not to *Listen*.

As is the case of having *Empathy* for our physical surroundings, it's not only humans who are worth *Listening* to for guidance on how to proceed toward success.

> **Listening is not just hearing somebody talk. It's taking action based on what they say.**

We should *Listen* to the past, such as the well-documented history of what happened during the pandemic of 1918. Since just about all the same things we went through from 2020 to 2022 already had happened more than one hundred years previously, did we *Listen* and learn from it? Clearly, not nearly enough.

PEC**PL**

PASSION

One of the most important overall themes of ***Get a Life*** is be ***Obsessed*** about everything and anything you want. It's not enough to just say you want it. I hear that all the time. You know what? No matter how much somebody says it, or how sincere they sound, or how loud they shout it, action speaks louder than words.

When you have ***Mentored*** and managed people for decades, you develop a sixth sense about who really wants it and who just gives lip service about wanting it. I can detect the difference after spending only a few minutes with someone.

My actor friend says when he, or any actor, auditions for a part, seasoned casting directors know in less than a minute if the actor is right for the role. So maybe I'm like a casting director in that sense because it doesn't take me very long either to size someone up before deciding if both of us will benefit from the mentorship. Do they really want to achieve to the max their dreams and goals or just *say* they do? Do they really *want* it?

Other key questions: Are they willing to *change* to get what they want? Or do they just want it to be *their* way? Do they bend the world to their will or adapt themselves to the world?

If you have substance and have the ***Passion*** to make the right connections, you got it made. But be aware that there's a kind of **Listening** that comes and goes quickly. That's not what I'm talking about here. My ***Passion*** never goes away. It's ***Relentless***.

Every time I push for something, I usually get it. Not to make a point but to make a difference. My wife, ***Stephanie***, sometimes asks why I do that if it stresses me out. It's because I feed on the stress, the challenges, the need to push myself to make things happen.

Some people say, "The sky is the limit." I say, "Who says it's the limit?" That's why my mantra is more optimistic than that: ***The Best Is Yet to Come!***

If you put a limit on it, you're immediately shortchanging your dreams. I see people put limits on themselves all the time. There are those who have decent careers but don't go as far as they envision. Why? Because they do more talking than doing. The ***Passion*** is in the action.

When I left ***rue21***, my ***Passion*** wasn't that I wanted a job or that I needed to build something and make it work. Been there, done that. My ***Passion*** was to find something in the world I could do that is gratifying to me and beneficial to others.

Money has never been a main motivation for me. Building something from scratch. Making a difference in somebody's life. That's my compensation—seeing that I helped people achieve more than they realized they could.

That's where ***FIT*** fits in my post-***rue21*** career. The heady feeling of exhilaration that ***rue21*** gave me for fifteen years is hard to replicate at this point, but I was willing to fight for achieving a new form of exhilaration.

My situation may have changed, going from CEO to entrepreneur, but my ***Passion*** never wavered. It still was there, as always.

After ***rue21***, I didn't have a billion-dollar corporation behind me, but in ***FIT*** I had a world-famous college in front of me. I was determined to make something happen between me and the school. It didn't happen quickly, and it took a lot of effort on both our parts. But my passion was strong enough to make it happen.

It's the *Art of the Possible*. It's standing up for what you believe is possible when others think it is impossible. It's believing in yourself. You can make something happen that others are convinced never could happen.

You have to study and understand what pushes people and how people push themselves. It's hard to explain, and it's even harder to teach. I can't give you *Passion*. You have to give it to yourself. You have to feel the burn inside you. (For tips on how to find your *Passion*, check *Brooke Carlson*'s comments in this chapter's *Rules of Reinvention*.

Are you *Passionate* in your belief that progress is possible only through change? Then you're *Passionate* about the rise of multiculturalism, the growing movement to tame climate change, renewable energy, and protecting human rights. Use your *Passion* not just to create your own success but also to help change the world.

CURIOSITY

I don't claim to be smarter than other people intellectually. My secret is that I am fearless in that I am not afraid to take a risk and not worried about the consequences.

I also am endlessly *Curious*. About people. I love to engage people in conversations, whether I know them or not. I ask them questions about themselves and figure out if there's some help I can offer.

I also like to learn how things work. When we were building our support center offices at *rue21*, I even knew how much poundage was required to flush the toilets we were installing. I'm *Curious* about the state of the world. I have cable news turned on continuously throughout the day to keep tabs on what's going on where and how it might affect me.

After I left *rue21*, someone who's known me a long time said, "I know you don't know what you will do now because *rue 21* was your life, but I know you always search for something meaningful, and if there's anyone on the planet I know can come up with doing something new and different, it's you."

I attribute it to my endless *Curiosity*. I search and search and search and don't stop until I find what I'm looking for. I don't really ever stop, actually. I just move on to the next adventure.

Curiosity is a cousin to *Empathy*. It takes an authentic thirst for knowledge. Along with *Humility* and the *Integrity* to know what you don't know. It's being *Curious* about other people and what makes them tick.

If you develop a healthy *Curiosity* about others, you'll have more *Empathy* for others. Because it's all about *PECPL: People. Empathy. Curiosity. Passion. Listening.*

PEOPLE

RULES OF REINVENTION

ARE YOU WARRIOR WORTHY?

Brooke Carlson calls herself a **Warrior**. She says it partly in jest. Yet as I've grown to know her and work with her closely while building my partnership with **Fashion Institute of Technology (FIT)**, where she oversees the School of Graduate Studies, **Warrior** is a good word to describe her.

I think of Brooke as someone who personifies the five traits featured in this chapter: **Patience**, **Empathy**, **Curiosity, Passion**, **Listening**.

I like the way Brooke links **Patience** with **Listening**.

Let's **Listen** to her wise words: "I learned how to be proactive yet **Patient** with myself at the same time. It meant not letting the impatience of others be put on to me. 'That's your impatience, not mine,' I would think to myself. 'That's how *you* feel.' Taking a breath in some situations has been really important for me. I often do breathing exercises so my mind can be clear and focused. It's stepping back for a minute, one hour, or one day and not feel pushed or compelled to blurt out an answer."

Listening, says Brooke, is essential to **Empathy**. "I have always believed in understanding where others are coming from." For her, that includes knowing how others "are feeling and how they work and function. **Empathy** helps me to adjust my approach by knowing where others are coming from."

Part of being a **Warrior** is seeking adventure. Brooke checks that box too. "I know I won't win every battle or succeed in every challenge, but I will put my all into it every single time," she says. "Adventure for me means **Curiosity** and learning. I'm always **Curious** about what will be next, **Curious** about how things function."

Brooke's Curiosity feeds her drive to work, which is her Passion. "Passion for me is all about loving to work. My working hard isn't for me. I like doing it for others. I find young people today don't have the same Passion. They don't see the opportunities the same way we did."

I asked Brooke how people like her and me, who both love to work with young people to see them succeed and thrive, can help instill Passion in them.

Brooke said, "Giving Opportunities to young people to experience different things is a way to discover where their true Passions lie. They might have more than one type of Passion or things they want to pursue. The world of work is changing. There will always be people who don't want one job tied to one company tied to one career.

"We can give people an opportunity to experience something even if they don't necessarily have the credentials for it yet, but they're willing to try and jump in. They need to have the drive to want to learn. I've always believed in continuous learning and continuous improvement. The Japanese word for that is Kaizen. Not everybody necessarily believes in that, but once you give them Opportunities for it, then I think they discover it, and that will lead them down that path to the Passion—hopefully."

EVERYBODY NEEDS A BUDDY!

TO EXCEL IN LIFE and in business, nothing is more valuable to your future than a *Mentor*—or more misunderstood.

If I were to ask "Who are your *Mentors*?" you might dig deep into your brain for names that live up to that specialized role.

You shouldn't really have to try that hard, though, to identify who the *Mentors* have been in your life up to now.

How about your parents? Siblings? Bosses? Teachers? Lovers? Mortal enemies? That's right. If you don't think you can learn a thing or two from people you otherwise might despise, think again.

That's what I mean by mentors being misunderstood—as a concept. They are not always wearing a badge or using a hashtag that says *#IAmaMentor*. You may consider someone who helps you to be your *Mentor*, but it doesn't mean they know they are *Mentoring* you.

Similarly, someone looking for life and career guidance doesn't have a hashtag that says *#PleaseMentorMe*. One reason for that is because simply asking someone you admire and respect to *Mentor* you is not enough. Not nearly enough. You must sell yourself as a worthy *Mentee*.

What's also misunderstood about *Mentoring* is that the person being *Mentored* may not immediately recognize the relationship exactly that way.

When an *FIT* student who sits in on one of my Fireside Chats I hold at the college asks me to *Mentor* them, part of me wants to look them square in the eye and ask, "What do you think I'm doing during the chats you've attended?"

I think of those chats as group *Mentoring* or mass *Mentoring* sessions. I'm sharing my experience and lessons I've learned with people starving for *Mentorship*. I take it very seriously and only want to mentor those who also are serious about improving themselves and who I can learn from. That's the essence of *Mutual Mentoring*.

"Mentorship is a lot of *Empathizing*," says my niece *Laura Littman*. "It's a *Mentor* like Bob telling someone that he's been in their situation and here's how he handled it. It's recognizing that a problem today was the same problem many years ago. It's a shared experience without judgment, not pontificating or reading a manual but finding commonalities across time."

HARD-WON PARTNERSHIPS

Of course there is much more to be gained through a one-to-one *Mentoring* relationship than mass *Mentoring*. Those are hard-won partnerships that cut both ways. Simply asking someone to mentor you sort of misses the point. You first have to prove to the person you are worth the time and energy they must invest to make the *Mentoring* mutually beneficial.

My friend *Jeff Erdmann* is a star in his field of wealth managers. He's a down-to-earth guy who doesn't go around bragging about himself, although he'd be well justified if he did. He's paid his dues. And he's done it simply by being smart and affable. Those can be powerful traits to have, as Jeff's singular success proves.

As a wealth manager at *Merrill*, he has landed the top spot for six years in a row on *Forbes* magazine's ranking of people in his profession. Jeff makes it a point to surround himself with high achievers. During his career he has worked with and trained thousands of people, many in their twenties to early forties.

Along the way he has learned a lot even as he has taught a lot. "Younger generations can get caught up with wanting instant answers. They need to remember to help others." He encourages mentees to ask questions of others. "Personal acknowledgment has gone by the wayside. What's most important is what matters to others, not yourself. Rapport building has been lost."

It's not unlike a doctor-patient relationship. The patient must be willing to follow the doctor's orders to support the healing process. Likewise, the *Mentored* person in the partnership must be willing to give as well as to receive if both sides are to extract value from the back-and-forth exchanges.

> Like anything else in life, collaboration makes each of us better by trading ideas, reinforcing each other, and disagreeing respectfully.

Like anything else in life, collaboration makes each of us better by trading ideas, reinforcing each other, and disagreeing respectfully, as long as you come to the table with well-considered reasons to justify your position.

There is even an element of **Reverse Mentoring** in that relationship because, to me, **Mentoring** someone is the most valuable experience I can learn from. It is my personal fountain of youth that never grows old.

When I have requests from **FIT** students to be mentored, their interest isn't limited to their academic studies. They see value in extending the **Mentorship** indefinitely as they strike out on their own in the business world, where finding a suitable **Mentor** is a major challenge.

At **rue21**, we practiced both mentoring and reverse mentoring. Our **rue21** Teen Board was composed of girls thirteen to seventeen years old. It's thanks to their recommendation that we added swimwear to our stores, which grew into a major revenue stream that increased our bottom line.

A mentee of mine whose fearlessness I admired is **Carrie Gaddy**. As one of hundreds of store managers at **rue21**, she was determined to break out of the pack. She took the lead on her own and boldly made her skills and value known to me. She subsequently was promoted to district manager in a Georgia store, where she became our number one district manager nationwide in three out of **rue21**'s four major sales categories. That is a remarkable achievement.

Carrie also made sure that I wasn't the only person of influence who recognized her worth. As a result, even after I left **rue21**, she made good use of my mentorship by impressing other executives. Her star continued to rise in the company. After **rue21**, Carrie became VP of Operations at **Smile Direct Club**.

"Bob has a real enthusiasm for the creative ideas of young people and a commitment to listening to them and empowering them to do their best work," said *FIT* President Dr. Joyce Brown when we announced my *FIT* scholarship program.

"What makes this partnership with Bob unique is that he is also donating his time and expertise," she continued, "something we highly value in the graduate school."

SHARED KNOWLEDGE

People are starved for *Mutual Mentorship*. There is value in learning the long-term vision of a *Boomer* and for *Boomers* to learn from *Millennials* or *Zoomers*. It requires an open mind for learning and mentoring. It's a balance of shared knowledge where everyone benefits.

My role at *FIT* includes motivating other *FIT* donors and board members to do the same. It's building a *Mentoring* model where the *Vision* is simple and easy to follow. It's giving back to pay it forward. That also sums up the psychic rewards of *Mentoring*.

I envision an ongoing *Mentoring* program among students and faculty members, as well as taking advantage of outside advisors like me, from the business world.

That idea could spin off into a stand-alone program, following the practice of other universities, such as the *Fordham Mentoring Program*. The program "carefully matches students with alumni *Mentors* based on commonalities in their personal and professional profiles."

A member of my *MAB*, who I also mentor, *Desiree "Dezz" Nunes*, is a *Fordham* alumna. "Bob always confronts me," she says, "and doesn't just 'yes' me. He tries to help me through constructive criticism." Through *Mutual Mentoring*, where I also listen intently to her, there also is mutual trust. She influences me, and I influence her.

It is through that model of *Mentoring* that my hope is for students to say they want to go to *FIT* because they think that the school's *Mentoring* curriculum will make an appreciable difference in their career aspirations.

That's already happening in the business world. Smart companies are using the perk of *Mentoring* to attract and keep top talent. It's also a great *Mutual* and *Reverse Mentoring* tool. Senior managers inside the organization can learn a lot from younger colleagues about consumer behavior among their peers, which in turn helps the company's marketing strategy.

Estée Lauder does that. So does *Google*. *Mentoring* is especially useful as an onboarding device to make new hires feel more comfortable and have a "buddy" assigned to them to answer questions and navigate the new environment, which can be very intimidating to entry-level workers. They typically are paired with someone who is highly relatable as far as background, personality, and functional responsibility. That increases the chances that the *Mentorship* will work for both and benefit the company, by grooming more effective and knowledgeable new employees.

My interest in *Mentoring* reaches back to the earliest days of my career in apparel retailing.

In my late twenties, while a merchandise manager at Jordan Marsh, I greatly enjoyed speaking to groups of my peers about how to get ahead. My talks addressed a range of real-life situations, such as how to get ahead when you can't relate to your boss or when you are saddled with a weak boss. Those classes I gave at Jordan Marsh formed the foundation of my affinity for *Mentoring*.

DO YOU LOVE WHAT YOU DO?

If you love what you do, it's easier to make the vision a reality. Are you doing what you really want to do?

As I started out in my retailing adventure, I felt I had discovered the best of both worlds. Tying together the victories of your professional life with the gratification of your personal life is a healthy balance that's worth striving to attain. You need to savor the joy of both for a full and purposeful existence.

As I tell the *FIT* graduate students, mentors don't grow on trees. You can't pick one like a piece of fruit.

What kind of person do you think will work best for you as a *Mentor*? You need to be in touch with your personality and how it will mesh with the *Mentor*. If you are ultrasensitive to criticism, for example, it's probably not a great idea to align yourself with someone who doesn't mince words or sugarcoat their comments. Although if you are that sensitive, you do need to grow a thicker skin, for your own sake. Like they say, *Honesty* is the best policy. You want *Honest* feedback at all times, even if it can sound harsh some of those times.

I always found that the best *Mentors* for me were people as aggressive as I was. I listened to them very intently and tried to learn. Even though I had these people around me, I still needed to attract their interest in counseling me.

Is the best *Mentor* for you the person who you feel is the most friendly or supportive of you? Yes and no. The strongest *Mentor* could be the person who confronts you or tries to push you past your ideal comfort level. It can be a very delicate balance between criticism that is constructive and insulting.

Not to generalize, but I find many *Millennials* in my orbit could do better accepting criticism and take it less personally. Feedback is not always going to be positive and all *kumbaya*, so get used to taking your lumps—and liking it. And by the way, don't be afraid to push back if you feel you need to defend your actions or your thinking.

That's part of the growth process of being *Mentored* and of *Reverse Mentoring* the *Mentor*.

Remember, just because you like someone more than another as your *Mentor* doesn't mean your favorite is your best choice. You may like them more, but that does not always make them the best *Mentors*. You benefit more from positive and negative reinforcement combined.

What better way to know which issues you most need to work on? A stronger *Mentor* will make you a stronger leader by saying what you need to hear, not only what you want to hear. The tougher person can be the best *Mentor* you ever had. Learn to be motivated by people who push you. Struggles help you prepare for the future.

GET PUSHED TO THE NEXT LEVEL

It's actually quite logical—a strong leader *Mentoring* you might make you a stronger leader by pushing you to the next level.

As mentioned earlier in this chapter, you can't merely ask your desired *Mentor* to fill that role for you. For one, odds are you're not the only one seeking their *Mentorship*. You have to prove to them what makes you special and unique. Remember that it's human nature for all of us to ask "What's in it for me?" That's what they'll be asking themselves when you ask them to be your *Mentor*. You need to have a compelling answer. How can you help them? That's where *Mutual Mentoring* and *Reverse Mentoring* enter the picture.

I want to *Mentor* someone who is obsessed with getting ahead. If you tell me that you can learn a lot from me, sure, that's flattering, but I'm not naive. Maybe you are trying as hard as you can. I don't doubt it. But is that the same as working as smart as you can? If there's anything more impressive than working fourteen hours a day to get ahead, it's working ten hours a day and being even more successful. Quantity isn't always quality. You have to show me why you want to be *Mentored*. You have to wow me.

FIT Dean *Brooke Carlson* told students that I respond most strongly to someone's "passion and drive to succeed." I like to force people as well as share my experience with them to help them achieve their dreams by being *Obsessed*, *Fearless*, and *Standing Up* for what they believe.

My style might best be described as *Motivational Mentoring*. Knowing what *Motivates* people is essential to helping them succeed, which in turn helps the company succeed and keeps them happy in their work. That propels the cycle of high achievement for everyone. Success breeds success, a maxim that was proven repeatedly as *rue21* recorded an extraordinary forty-five consecutive quarters—eleven years—of never missing a sales and profit projection.

You also should be asking yourself, what's in it for you? It's okay to be selfish about being mentored and to say to yourself "I need a *Mentor* to get ahead."

For the longest time, billionaire *Mark Cuban*, of popular CNBC TV series *Shark Tank*, was known as being indifferent to *Mentoring*. Yet on a January 2022 episode, he told a nineteen-year-old entrepreneur that his $400,000 investment in her start-up was contingent on her *Mentoring* his two young daughters. That's the power of *Mentoring*.

When done right, and when it's working really well, another benefit of *Mentoring* is the multiplier effect it creates, linking you to the influencers within the *Mentor*'s orbit.

IT'S WHO YOU KNOW

That kind of networking generates connections, which are as good as gold when climbing your career ladder. That's how you get ahead and get jobs. It would be nice to think that talent speaks for itself and gets you hired for the job you covet. It also would be foolish to think that. More often than not, with two or more people of comparable qualifications and desirability to the recruiter, the one who comes recommended by someone inside or close to the company will walk away with the gig.

I used a hypothetical example for the *FIT* students: I told them that I travel a lot, which connects me with a wide range of high-powered entrepreneurs and CEOs. If one of the students said they want to learn from me as a *Mentor* and that they need connections, maybe I can speak to one of these people as a way for the student to get their foot in the door. That expression "It's who you know" is not just empty words. Trust me, it's a fact of life.

It's not news that we live in challenging times, arguably unlike any era in recent memory. Even for *Baby Boomers*, who have lived through assassinations, recessions, domestic terrorism, and constant wars, the extreme adversity created by the pandemic has no equal.

Our new age of anxiety is especially unnerving to *Millennials* and younger, who have no playbook for how to deal with the constant setbacks they face in every part of their lives—job security, financial insecurity, relationships, social isolation.

That sense of despair is a major reason why this book was written. More than ever, it takes a certain superpower to cope and overcome negativity in our surroundings.

I believe part of the answer to how we can heal ourselves—and each other—is through *Mental Mentoring*.

The pandemic effectively stole two years from our lives. There are stories from teachers of fifth-grade students stuck at a third-grade reading level because of the constant disruption of regular classwork and homework. For a young worker stuck at home instead of at an office desk, how could they be *Mentored* toward a promotion?

For someone in their first job, almost 10 percent of their life was virtually imprisoned by the pandemic. How can that not change people's lives for the long term?

With psychological and emotional health endangered to that serious extent, regardless of age, the need for human connection is heightened to the max. With everyone on edge, and having faith that there is strength in numbers, it's fair to say that we all are candidates for *Mental Mentoring*.

In fact, a case can be made that the pandemic forms an inflection point where *Mental Mentoring*, *Mutual Mentoring*, *Reverse Mentoring*, and even *Motivational Mentoring* all converge.

In that way, *Mentoring* becomes an all-purpose remedy for what ails us. When you see someone with pain, make it your business to need to reach out to them. We all will benefit from good advice, however young or old the advisor may be.

For the 117th session of Congress (January 2021–January 2023), half of the U.S. Senate was over the age of sixty-five. I often wonder how much *Mentoring* junior members receive from the senior members and vice versa. Our politicians, especially those in the upper reaches age-wise, need to get over themselves and get to work on some serious *Mutual Mentoring*.

With *Millennials* and *Gen Z* poised to take over the world, we need to help them on their way, not get in their way.

RULES OF REINVENTION

HEY, BUDDY, CAN YOU HELP ME OUT?

- These thoughts are meant to help you wrap your mind around the multidimensional meaning and uses of *Mentoring*.

- Keep in mind that there are no right or wrong answers here. Only *Your* answers.

- What are your *Values* in how you treat people and how you want to be treated?

- What *Values* do you want in your *Mentor*?

- What *Value* do you bring to your *Mentor*?

- What is the best way to find the *Mentor* who is right for you?

- Does your company or university have a formal *Mentoring* program?

- Has a *Mentor* ever saved you from making a terrible decision?

- What is the multiplier effect of *Mentoring*?

- Do you think *Mentoring* can change the course of your life?

- What lessons about *Mentoring* did the pandemic teach you?

- Do you have what it takes to be a *Mentor* or be *Mentored*?

ROADMAP TO THE REST OF YOUR LIFE

"And if you should survive to 105, look at all you'll derive out of being alive..." *

LET'S FACE IT, 105 is the new 85! No matter what age you are, that's good news. Someone who today is, say, 40 can expect to live at least another couple of lifetimes compared with past life spans.

I easily could have rested on my laurels in my fifties. Instead, my most rewarding years in business, and in life, came after that, and there is no letup in sight!

What's my secret? ***Always look ahead. Plan for the future.*** Create a ***Roadmap*** to the rest of your life. Don't lock yourself into the false and dangerous narrative that your best days are behind you or that you have to blossom right now. Stop pressuring yourself that if you don't succeed by thirty, you're failing in your life's work. That's self-defeating nonsense! Says who? Me.

I listen to people who I respect for their *Smarts* and *Honesty* and *Authenticity*. But mostly, in the end, I listen to myself. Who am I? Who do I want to be? Who do you want to be? Are you listening to yourself?

Planning for the future means preparing to enjoy longer, more productive lives than past generations could imagine. That's because dramatic progress in healthcare, as well as in our lifestyle choices, keeps extending our longevity.

Consider my great-nephew *Jacob Littman*, who will be a spry eighty-one by the time the twenty-second century rolls around. Based on what we know today, it's not at all inconceivable that, eight decades from now, someone Jacob's age will continue to be highly productive at that stage of life.

It's entirely possible to envision that the Jacobs of the future may not slow down until they are well past one hundred! At that point who's to say they won't be active in a second, or third, or even fourth career?

Thanks to my *MAB*, I appreciate firsthand that *Millennials* place less importance than *Boomers* on such values as owning a home and staying at one job for a long time and put more value on their *Happiness* and *Freedom*.

There's nothing wrong with that as long as they have *Patience* in putting together the *Pieces of the Puzzle* in their lives. Where some *Millennials* do go wrong is assuming that they are at peak performance in their thirties or forties. In the framework of the new *Longevity*, what is middle age anyhow? Does it even matter?

YOUR FUTURE LIVES

I was just getting started in my thirties and forties, so don't freak out if you're not master of the universe by your thirties or forties. By the yardstick of what used to be called *middle age*, at forty, you still have a long, rich road to plow ahead of you. There's plenty of time to ascend the throne in one of the future lives you build for yourself. As my book attests, I'm living proof of that. I'm **Patient** when I need to be—as in planning for the future—and impatient when that works for me. How about you?

Never count yourself out when you have an obsession that burns inside you. I've known this book's ghostwriter, **Bruce Apar**, since junior high school. He had planned to major in acting. In fact, one of his college classmates was **Sylvester Stallone**. Bruce's path after college took a different turn, though, and he was very happy pursuing a gratifying writing career. Then as he was approaching what used to be considered retirement age, he thought to himself, "Who says I can't become an actor now?" And so he did just that! Now he's both a writer and an actor. He drew and then redrew the road-map to the rest of his life. It can be done at any age because age shouldn't make a difference.

What about you?

Is there a future you trapped inside of you? The future you I'm talking about is who you want to be but aren't confident how you get there. How do you find that person? How do you reach the future *you* … sooner than later? In a word, **Liberation**. You need to **Liberate**

> **Never count yourself out when you have an obsession that burns inside you.**

yourself. You need to go after what you think you can do to make something happen.

To do that, you need to figure out what will **Liberate** you. It may not be the same thing that liberates someone else, whether it's your spouse or child or friend. You have to do you! To do that, you need to understand you. Do you? Know your comfort zone, and step outside it.

What I'm talking about here is your **Alter Ego**. It's there, believe me. One of the most insightful activities I undertook at **rue21** was an **Alter Ego** party. My intention was to encourage our associates to burst out of their comfort zone and fantasize about the "what-ifs" of business and life. That can be a very powerful role-playing game. It provides a window into a person's innermost desires.

ALTER EGO PARTY

Bob with Lynne Lindley at
the Alter Ego party

One of our **rue21** people came to the **Alter Ego** party as Wonder Woman. Another envisioned herself as legendary racehorse Secretariat! She showed up outfitted with a tail and with a large jockey doll strapped to her back. Part of the fun is just seeing how creative people can be when they are pushed to use their imagination.

It was fascinating to see how it also could work the other way, where someone with a loud personality at work showed up at the *Alter Ego* party as a low-key teacher or librarian. That created its own exciting element of surprise, as if the person wanted to tell us "You don't really know me as well as you think."

You can see your personal possibilities more clearly when you look at yourself through a different lens. By acting out your *Alter Ego* in front of other people, you also can see their reaction—good, bad, or indifferent.

My *Alter Ego* at the party was *Maroon 5* and *The Voice* star *Adam Levine*. I felt I had to set an example for the rest of the company, so I wasn't satisfied just wearing a costume and leaving it at that. I actually shed fifteen pounds to wear skinny jeans and a tank top. As the finishing touch, tattoos were hand-painted on both arms.

At the core of my *Mentoring* philosophy and style is to push people to their limits and to pull out of them their best selves. That's not who I want them to be. That's who they want to be but need a spark to light their fire. I'm the spark.

I was fortunate to run businesses where I felt that way about wanting to help people. How do you do it now? In managing and *Mentoring* people and building businesses, I've identified several factors holding people back. Lack of *Motivation* is one. You can't rely on a boss or coworker or even a family member or close friend to *Motivate* you. They can help, but it has to start and end with you *Self-Motivating*.

I was a leader who challenged people not only in matters of business but also on a personal level. I feel they tie in together and that I could help them improve both sides of their *Identity*. It doesn't mean they have to always be mirror images of each other. I wanted to point out how one can inform the other in good ways. If I sensed someone didn't have the desire to change, I didn't push them. Why bother? You only should push people who want to change but are afraid to.

When I met with employees or job candidates at companies I ran, sometimes I would conduct an exercise to help them identify their *Alter Ego*. (*See Rules of Reinvention at the end of this chapter*.)

RISK-TAKER OR RISK-AVERSE?

On a blank piece of paper, I drew a straight horizontal line at the top, from left to right. I labeled the left end of the line *Comfort Zone* and the right end *Risk-Taker*.

Then I asked the person two questions:

1. "Where are you on this chart in your private life?"

2. "Where are you on this chart in your business life?"

One district manager pointed to the left side of the line, saying, "This is where I am in my private life," meaning she saw herself hiding in her *Comfort Zone*. Then pointing to the far right side of the line, she added, "But here is where I want to be," meaning she longed to be more adventurous.

I would ask these same people, "What stops you from breaking out of your *Comfort Zone*?"

Invariably, the most frequent responses were "My family" or being afraid to take risks.

I then asked if the same shyness about breaking out of their shell applied as well to their work colleagues—their business family—and they would say yes to that too.

One of my *Mentees* has acknowledged having that kind of fear of being her true self in her work life. It's a fear of being criticized for being bold or opinionated in front of coworkers and supervisors. I get upset when I hear that because that fear of self can hold back very talented people.

Hiding your true aura can undermine job performance and, worse, diminish the impact and earning power of your entire career. It's basically a *Fear of Success (see chapter 10)*. You know you want to follow your impulses, but your *Comfort Zone* won't let you. That's deadly. The best way to fight fear in this respect is to keep having your fear challenged. That's what I set out to do with those I *Mentor*.

Some people avoid getting tattoos because it would be looked down on in their conservative workplace. Tattoos are not going to make you a success or a failure, but they symbolize who you want to be. If you shrink from getting tattooed because you're concerned that others in your place of work will look at you with disdain, you're letting others control your life.

A lot of people in their twenties and thirties pointed to their family as holding them back from being who they truly wanted to be. "What would my family think of me if I moved or changed my appearance?" was not an uncommon remark I would hear. I would come back by asking, "If you no longer lived in the same town as your family, moving to a new town, and making new friends, then how would you be?"

"I'd be totally different" was a typical response to that question. So I'd say, "Then why don't you do that now?" I wonder, though, if moving away from your family is the answer. Your surroundings might change, but you still would be you.

How much would a new living environment dramatically change you? In running away from your geography, are you really moving away from your current self to remake yourself in a new image? That comes from a change that's made inside your head, not from a change of address.

ONE PERSON, TWO PERSONAS

The equally significant insight gleaned from the **Comfort Zone vs. Risk-Taker** exercise is how many of us have two personas—one in our work life and a different one in our personal life.

Someone might point to the **Risk-Taker** end of the spectrum as their private persona but to the opposite side of the line, **Comfort Zone**, as their business persona. I always marvel at—and am frustrated by—the sharp contrast in a person who acts fearless on their own time but doesn't bring that **Fearlessness** to work every day. I almost feel as if I'm being shortchanged by that employee. Give me that **Fearlessness**. Bring it on!

The objective is to blend your business persona and private persona in a way that combines the best and strongest elements of both into one great person.

In fact, you would benefit from running your life like a business. There's a saying that **Discipline** is liberating. While the very word **Discipline** might suggest demanding or intimidating behaviors such as focus and time management, the effect ends up being the opposite. **Discipline** gives you more time to excel, to enjoy, to expand your ambition and your opportunities. **Discipline** and doing something out of the ordinary is "taking control" of your life when you do something that is a risk. When I did something risky, I was motivated by needing to regain control. **Discipline** and doing something out of the ordinary is "taking control" of your life. It's like a shock to the system that energizes you like a bolt of lightning.

The form of **Discipline** I'm talking about here that should run your life as it runs a business is strategy. Do you have one? How far ahead do you project and plan? Ten years? Thirty years? Fifty? That's the **Roadmap to the Rest of Your Life**. Ask yourself if ten years from now, you still will be searching for what you want or deciding who you want to be.

Like my actor friend, it's okay if you are because it means you always are thinking about the roadmap and where you want it to take you on your next journey. Never stop exploring new paradigms to redefine your essence. Whatever your game plan is, remember that it's not a contradiction to be both **Ambitious** and **Realistic** about it.

There are people who have decent careers but also don't go as far as they envision and talk about. Do they really want to achieve to the max their dreams and goals, or are they mostly talk? Do they really want it badly enough to change what's holding them back? Do they just want it to be their way? Do you bend the world to your will or adapt yourself to the world? Or both?

I'm known for my blunt approach to **Mentoring** people. I don't waste my time or anyone else's by tiptoeing around what needs to be said.

It's easy to say you need a **Roadmap to the Rest of Your Life**, but how do you go about finding the path that serves you best and leads to whatever goals you set for yourself?

I think of it as several maps. There's the macro roadmap, which is an aerial view of the milestones you create for your life. Then there are micro roadmaps to get you to each of those milestones, one leg of the trip at a time.

You can break it down even more into a day-to-day roadmap. Did you accomplish today what you set out to do and needed to do to move you along toward your destination? Thinking that way is the only way to achieve consistent progress. **Consistency** is one of the mantras I live by. Are you setting your goals consistently to succeed?

You must drill down into manageable pieces of work and time to draw your **Roadmap** and set its course, according to your true north.

What helped me immensely in my career is that even though I did have a fear of taking **Risks** on a personal level, the amount of fear I had taking **Risks** in business was always a big, fat zero. No fear at all in that part of my life. I also was **Fearless** in playing out my business persona, yet the same wasn't always true of my personal life, at least not until now. I am as **Fearless** in everything I do as I always was in business.

I **Motivate** myself by **Motivating** others. That's my thing. I ran my companies like a big family, and the energy that came back to me pushed me further toward my goals. By showing how much I was concerned about their personal lives—and not just their nine-to-five lives—they didn't want to let me down, and I didn't want to let them down. People would come into my office to proudly talk about a special accomplishment. That kind of worker pride and dedication is as good as it gets for a CEO and for the people whose livelihoods depend on his or her commitment to corporate growth and prosperity.

CONTROL YOUR DESTINY

Another key part of my strategy has been something I emphatically *don't* do. I don't care what people think of my decisions or actions that are taken in the interest of building a business and being a **Fearless** competitor who leads by example. I want people to jump high, not to be a CEO necessarily but to control their own destiny, whether the domain they rule is their company or somebody else's.

At Jordan Marsh, I created new categories of business that set the tone for other stores around the country. I always was interested in doing what's best for the people I answer to, whether that's the corporation or the customer buying our goods.

As a lifelong basketball fan, my role models are legendary coaches such as **Red Auerbach** because they also are great leaders who create championship teams. To get to that level, you must take **Risks** and not be afraid to fail. That only holds you back. When I talk to people, they understand what it takes, but that doesn't mean they can flip a switch and do it. Very few can do it. They get scared.

I'm not smarter than anyone else intellectually. I was just **Fearless**, unafraid to take a **Risk** and not worried for a minute about losing my job. Whenever I confronted someone who was a threat to me and pushed back harder than they poked me, I always made sure there was someone mentoring me who would have my back. They wouldn't take my side just because I asked them to or because I needed them to.

It was because I had **Produced** for them. I added value to their part of the business and elevated their performance through mine. In business, relationships are transactional, so if you're not producing at or preferably above expectations, don't expect anybody to have your back for very long.

Whenever I feel the need for **Reinvention**, my path to it is through **Liberation**. After **rue21**, I set in motion a five-year **Roadmap** that started with my first book, **Fisch Tales: The Making of a Millennial Baby Boomer**, which expanded into the **Millennial Baby Boomer®** brand, **Mentoring** and endowing a scholarship program at **FIT**, and now this book sequel. Next on my **Roadmap** is a project involving the Miami Heat professional basketball team.

It is through that sequence of events that I **Liberated** myself from the business of retailing, pivoting away from that paradigm to a totally new paradigm of author, mentor, speaker, philanthropist, board member. One way to think of those times when, like me, you need something new to turn to is that they are the rest stops on the

Roadmap to the Rest of Your Life. That's where you feed your mind and fuel your body. Are you strategizing to feed your mind and fuel your body? You should if you aren't already.

When I needed to release tension that had built up from building *rue21* to a nationwide chain, my *Liberation* was weight loss. In six months, I went from 234 to a svelte 177—57 pounds lighter. The funny part is that I suddenly was so fashionable in my skinny jeans, designer T-shirt, and buzz cut that a flight attendant took me for a hairdresser.

DRESS FOR SUCCESS

The transformation extended to my daily wardrobe and my overall persona. I can't fully explain how great it made me feel that I was seen in a new light throughout the company and industry. The new me made enough of an impression in the garment center that coworkers decided to do the same and diet away the pounds.

Going back to the *Comfort Zone vs. Risk-Taker* chart, personal changes can result in positive business performance, and business success can influence your personal behavior, bolstering *Confidence* in other parts of your life. Who and what are your influences?

Even today, as much as ever, I want to be in the pulse of being *Fearless* about anything I do. It's not a lot different than as if I was still at *rue21*. I need to push myself as I push others. I need to practice what I preach. I have a hard time not constantly thinking about what to do next.

My meditation is jumping out of bed in the middle of the night for an hour or two and considering all the possibilities awaiting me in the day ahead. I feel really comfortable inside. My thoughts turn to how I want to reinvent myself again.

You don't want to be one of those people who hold on to things you really don't need to hold on to. When people change, 90 percent of the time, they feel good about it. Most people don't regret they changed. Neither will you.

That's why when planning the **Roadmap to the Rest of Your Life**, it's okay to allow for detours and to take advantage of those **Liberating** rest stops I talked about so you can keep the pedal to the metal when you're running low on fuel.

You need to take yourself further than you ever thought possible. The sky is the limit!

Personal changes can result in positive business performance, and business success can influence your personal behavior, bolstering *Confidence* in other parts of your life.

---

* **"Young at Heart" lyrics by Carolyn Leigh, music by Johnny Richards (pg. 99)**

RULES OF REINVENTION

ARE YOU WHERE YOU WANT TO BE?

| CONSERVATIVE COMFORT ZONE RISK AVERSE | ◀ ■ ■ | 🐟 | ■ ■ ▶ | RISK TAKER FEARLESS DISRUPTOR |

- Where are you in your life? Where do you want to go?

- Where are you in your career? Where do you want to go?

- The very simple diagram on this page is one way I motivate people to step outside themselves to see the possibilities— and, more important, the *Opportunities*—for upping their game in life and in business.

- If someone points to the right side of the chart as describing their private persona (*Risk-Taker*, *Fearless*, *Disruptor*) and then points to the left side as their work persona (*Conservative*, *Comfort Zone*, *Risk-Averse*), I ask that person why they wouldn't want to be a Risk-Taker at work too?

- It also works conversely. In other words, if you're *Risk-Averse* in your personal life and a *Disruptor* at your job, maybe you should consider finding a balance between those two to smooth out your work persona and liven up your private persona.

- The true inner you that coworkers don't see is your *Alter Ego*. The ideal you is a blend of the two yous. Your *Roadmap* needs to take that integrated vision of yourself into account because that's the person who will be driving you to your many destinations!

LEAD, FOLLOW, OR GET OUT OF THE WAY!

THERE IS HARDLY a day that goes by in my life where I'm not *Disrupting* something. It's nothing new for me. I've always been that way. If you think that's some kind of quirk, maybe it is. It's also my key to success. I credit that personality trait to just about all that I have accomplished in life and in business.

There's no mystery to why I'm like that. I just can't let something I consider wrong take place in front of me without taking action on it. I need to call it to attention and ask for it to be fixed.

"Ask" might be an understatement. It's more of a demand. And you know what? I usually get my way in the end. Even that might be an understatement. I almost always change the wrong into a right. Not just for me but also for others who may experience the same frustration but are too shy or just unwilling to confront the daily problems we all face.

My friend likes to tease me about my animated behavior at the NBA's Miami Heat home games, where I have season seats. I take my basketball seriously, and I take those seats seriously. So when fans casually hang out in the aisle, blocking my view of the court action, I stand up, my arms start flailing, and I yell at them to move or sit or just get out of my way.

There is an usher standing in front of the human obstacles, whose job it is to keep the area clear, but I was doing more to manage crowd control than I felt she was. She's very nice, but at that time, she was new to the job. She clearly wasn't being properly trained on how to keep stragglers moving along to not block sightlines. Training is management's job, so I didn't blame her. Still, I couldn't continue standing by without saying something to her. So I did. I was very nice about it. I didn't want to blame her. I wanted to help her and, by doing so, help me and other frustrated fans trying to watch the game unimpeded.

TAKE CONTROL

I quietly told her how to get in the pulse of her new job. The key phrase is *Take Control*. That's one of my mantras for everything I do. I think it should be everybody's mantra. At least everybody who wants to control their own destiny.

After that mini-*Mentoring* session, the usher was noticeably more assertive with fans. I went back to tell her "You're doing a great job." She went from a deer in the headlights to firmly telling people, "You can't be here."

I felt I had made a difference, a goal that's part of my daily routine. How about you? Like anything else in life, collaboration makes each of us better by exchanging ideas, reinforcing each other, and disagreeing respectfully and with reasons to back up your stance.

That's what I mean by being a *Disruptor*. It's not the old meaning that had negative connotations of making things worse. It means improving a situation by identifying the problem and figuring out the most efficient way to solve it. With the old meaning, those people clogging up the aisle would be called disruptors (with a small *d*!). They slow down progress or just screw up a situation and make it more stressful for everybody. Today they are known as *Interruptors*.

Disruptors are *Innovators*. *Movers and Shakers*. Think *Apple's Steve Jobs*, *Amazon's Jeff Bezos*, *Tesla's Elon Musk*. Master *Disruptors* all! They weren't satisfied changing entire industries. Their vision was to change the world! And they did. Being a *Disruptor* means going against the flow. You're more likely to uncover new ideas and fewer competitors; otherwise, you'd be going with the flow.

Being a *Disruptor* means you are not running with the pack. You are either running way ahead of the pack or running in the opposite direction, looking to blaze new trails like the intrepid American pioneers who found new frontiers for others to follow. They were *Disruptors* too.

Interruptors get in the way of *Disruptors*. Maybe they are contrarian and disagree for the sake of it. Maybe they are afraid of being left behind if they can't keep up with the energy and creativity of the

> **Being a Disruptor means you are not running with the pack. You are either running way ahead of the pack or running in the opposite direction, looking to blaze new trails.**

Disruptor. They tie everybody up, often for no good reason. *Interruptors* stall, moving sideway or backward. I have no use for them, period. I don't trust them. Neither should you.

There's a third group. I call them *Spectators*. They watch what's going on, size up the situation, then decide which way is the smart way to go. They are not *Risk-Takers*, to say the least.

Look at it this way: The *Disruptor* acts. The *Interruptor* reacts. The *Spectator* spectates.

DISRUPTORS ONLY

By now, you know who this book is not for. That's right. It's *Not for the Timid*. That's why it's also not for anybody but the *Disruptor*. *Disruptors* are not *Timid*.

I am so convinced about the overwhelming benefits of playing *Disruptor* that I don't see it as a matter of choice. It is a matter of necessity. If you're not getting what you want and you feel you deserve, is there any option other than shake up the status quo and bend it to your will?

My tendency to *Disrupt* the conventional way of doing things is not a forced behavior. It's more like an unconscious impulse I have that has served me very well.

In one of my earliest retail positions, at *Jordan Marsh* Miami, I gravitated toward regularly using the executive washroom, which was strictly reserved for those above my managerial level. Did I get some suspicious looks from senior managers as if to say "What do you think you're doing here?" Of course. Did I care? Of course not. Why should I? It's a stupid bathroom. As it turned out, they could have played *Interruptor*, but for some reason they never called me on invading their turf.

I didn't do it just to be a smart-ass. That form of *Disruption* paid considerable dividends. There were confidential financial reports on the front desk on the way to the washroom. I helped myself to that valuable data to educate myself, keep on top of the company's overall sales performance, and stay one step ahead of my peers. By busting out of my lane, my brashness and resourcefulness in doing that was mentioned by the president when he promoted me eighteen months later. *Knowledge* is power!

If you think that's extreme behavior you can't relate to, like I said, my style is not for the *Timid*, and neither is this book.

Being a *Disruptor* is a way to keep you top of mind with the people who matter to you, the people who can help you progress in whatever way suits your goals and agenda. If you are expecting an answer from someone, or a deliverable on a job, and they are lagging, let them know they are late with what they promised you.

As with the Miami Heat usher, there's no need to be unpleasant about it, but there is a need to be firm and clear about it. Ask them to be specific about the date of delivery and then hold them to it. They may resent you for it. Tough. Don't worry if there are those who resent you for it. Accept the fact that not everybody will love you for being a *Disruptor*. It doesn't mean they still won't respect you.

OUTSPOKEN BUT RESPECTFUL

I bring my constructively *Disruptive* ways to business meetings I attend as well. If I feel a company or a project is heading in the wrong direction, I don't hesitate to speak right up. At the same time, I am respectful of others in the process.

True, it is not always easy to get your point across forcefully yet respectfully. It's a fine line to navigate. *Disruptors* have to walk between not suggesting to the others in the meeting that they are wrong or misguided and yet at the same time convincing them you happen to have specific experience they can take advantage of for the good of the business.

There also are times when you may not be assigned the job that needs to be done or the official title that goes with that job. The trouble is you see that the person who is supposed to take care of that job is not getting it done right or at all. What do you do? You *Disrupt*! You rush in where others fear to go and take care of business. *Disruptors* don't wait around for slowpokes or laggards. They see an opportunity, and they jump on it before it slips away.

Even your choice of communication can make a difference. I am much more interested in meeting with someone in person than talking with them by phone or Zoom. I am much more insistent in speaking with someone on the phone than in corresponding by email or text. *Disruptors* thrive on direct, real-time contact because they respect the importance of being timely and having immediate and empathetic human connection.

We don't evade. We engage, with almost military precision. *Discipline* is a critical tool in a *Disruptor*'s toolbox. It's like having a knife that cuts through the bullshit. That's the sharpest knife you can have. With so much going on that can hold you back or set you back, you need to machete your way through the jungle of junk that gets in our way every day.

As noted, there inevitably will be those you work with who don't react well to such a show of confidence, but letting it roll off your back is part of the *Disruptor* playbook. If you don't already have a thick skin, take my advice and grow one.

GROW A PAIR!

I find that the younger generation, who I mentor, can find it especially difficult to grow a pair. They don't understand that you have to go out of your way to push to have people understand you. Just because you are helping them doesn't mean they will see it that way. People are easily threatened by good ideas, especially if it's not theirs. (Remember the *Interruptor*?) You also need to concentrate on thinking out of the box, and that can put people on edge, afraid to escape the *Comfort Zone* that *is* the box.

To succeed at *Disrupting*, it's crucial to get people to see your vision for themselves. That's actually the easy part. Once you have buy-in, you need to make the vision a reality by taking it across the finish line, which is harder than getting investment in your idea from others.

Doing that is a tough challenge for young people who don't have enough tolerance or *Patience* to stare down the hard work it takes to build something worthwhile, whether it's a start-up of their own or a career working for others. It starts with believing in yourself. You can make something happen that people would think never could happen. I push people, including former employees I still am in close touch with, to help them climb their career ladder to the top. I study what pushes people and how people push themselves. Good things don't happen to you by magic. They don't happen if you don't push. On one hand, you can't get far without taking **Risks**. On the other hand, they should be smart, calculated **Risks** based on research, not crazy, careless **Risks** that are unstudied.

You have to sell your ideas. Life is one big sales call. Communicate and explain your ideas. It's not enough to just pitch your ideas. You also must convince people to understand your brainstorms in a way that relates to them so they think it is important and relevant and even helpful to achieving their goals as well as yours.

There is the rare time when my head says, "**Disrupt** this!" but I know better than to act on that impulse in the moment because it's not the right time or place. One time, at a state-of-the-industry symposium, it bothered me having to sit there and listen to one speaker after another talk trash about bricks-and-mortar retailing. To me, they were not **Disruptors**. They were **Interruptors**, spouting fake hype about start-ups that I knew had no chance of succeeding. But they were the shiny new thing, which can blind people who don't take the time to think things through carefully.

I knew they didn't know what they were talking about, and I so wanted to get up on stage and yell, "Stop the negativity!" but of course that would not go over well.

A certain trend is spotted, and **Interruptors** quickly jump on the bandwagon as if everything else that previously existed is now obsolete. They go to extremes instead of realizing that change doesn't happen overnight. It's a marathon, not a sprint. As I say in **Back to the Future** (chapter 11), the best way to get ahead—and **Get a Life**—is to hold on to the best practices of the past and enhance them with new techniques and technology that serve as helpful **Disruptors**.

What you don't do is abruptly throw away everything that has worked so well. Don't be fooled into allowing the next big thing to blind you to the lasting value of proven business models, such as bricks-and-mortar stores.

BAD IS NOT GOOD

As much as acting the *Disruptor* has become a popular method for breaking new ground and making progress, old forms of *Disruption* are still hanging around. When that gets in my way, my response is to meet bad disruption with good *Disruption*!

Where I live in Manhattan, in 2019 there was disruption that started going on right outside my apartment that I decided to respond to by *Disrupting* back.

Commutes to work were being *Disrupted*. Businesses were being *Disrupted*. Nearby streets were being *Disrupted* with detoured traffic.

The city of New York had launched an eighteen-month pilot program that banned cars sixteen hours a day along a one-mile stretch of bustling 14th Street.

Only buses, trucks, and emergency vehicles were permitted. The goal was to speed the time it takes public transportation (buses) to make the trip across town. I can understand that, but everything has its cost: what was supposed to be great for bus drivers and riders was grating on everybody else.

I don't drive a car in the city, so the ban didn't *Disrupt* me as a motorist. It did *Disrupt* me, though, any time I needed a taxi or car service, which couldn't pick us up in front of our building.

The day before the new traffic regulations went into effect, I was walking in my neighborhood when I saw a cluster of activity nearby. It turned out to be the New York City commissioner of transportation, holding a press conference, right on 14th Street, facing TV cameras and microphones from local TV stations.

MAN ON THE STREET

When people started asking questions, I did too, because I was concerned about the impact of the new rules. It didn't even occur to me that only reporters were allowed to ask questions in this informal outside setting. Someone in the commissioner's entourage tried to stop me from talking. I felt bad for them. They clearly didn't know they were dealing with a lifetime *Disruptor*!

I simply said the city should be diligent about closely tracking how effective the new hours would prove to be. I said they should track the activity during the banned hours to make adjustments along the way that would open the road to more vehicles over time.

My *Disruptive* behavior caught the attention of TV reporters. I appeared on the evening news in the country's biggest media market. By speaking up—out of turn, as a nonjournalist—my impromptu suggestion ended up reaching a far greater number of people than I expected.

That's what being a *Disruptor* means: You don't accept the status quo. You challenge it, undaunted by barriers that sometimes need to be knocked down so you can stand up for what you believe and what you want to achieve.

If I'm the *Disruptor* in that story, can you identify who is the *Interruptor* and who is the *Spectator*? (The answer is at the end of this chapter.)

Someone I admire who's a master *Disruptor* is *Joe De Sena*. He's hosted a show on CNBC called *No Retreat: Business Bootcamp* and is founder and CEO of *Spartan*, the world's

> **That's what being a *Disruptor* means: You don't accept the status quo. You challenge it.**

leading endurance sports and wellness brand, reaching a community of more than ten million people.

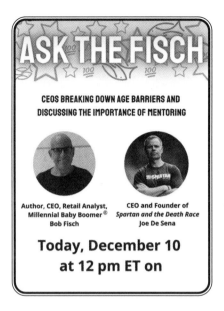

Spartan helps people "tear down boundaries and expand what they believe possible." That's another way of saying Joe pushes people, like I do, to be a ***Disruptor***.

On the inaugural episode of my podcast ***Ask the Fisch***, Joe talked about character building. Joe's bluntness and perceptive observations almost sound like it's me talking. We share many of the same values about how people need to overcome fear to blast past the limitations they set on themselves, especially with younger generations.

"There's a tremendous fear with our children today," says Joe.

WHERE'S THE GRIT?

"They don't have that grit or resilience or know how to negotiate on the street for a game of football."

Joe grew up in Queens and understands as well as anyone how important it is in a rough-and-tumble street culture to hustle if you want to hold your own and break out to create a worthwhile legacy, as he has done in a huge way.

I'm a very early riser. So is Joe. We both know you have to get a head start each day to make the most of every minute. In his neighborhood, Joe was up early, "getting after it." His street toughness was tested early on when he came into contact with organized crime.

"The number one attribute anybody can have is the ability to communicate, to sell who you are talking to," he says. "You're selling your ideas all day long." If that sounds familiar, it's because you just read the same thing I said a couple of pages before in this chapter.

Joe believes anything is possible. "I embrace failure. I don't look backwards. I wanted to make it and get to Manhattan to be with the big boys and girls. There are no obstacles you can't overcome. Why can't I go to Wall Street? My dad said everybody's the same. Have confidence. So I built a trading firm on Wall Street. Then I got disgusted with it."

A Navy SEAL told Joe, "If you want to one hundred times your life, do some form of exercise, sweating, and make sure you keep tight connections and relationships. It's a pretty simple system. Just put your head down, and believe in yourself. You got to take care of yourself. We get punched in the face every day in business. To stay healthy, your instincts may be to get a cookie, but you need to get a celery stick."

I love the way Joe graphically illustrates his "take no prisoners" gung ho spirit. "In the old days, when guns were created, it was ready, aim, fire," he says. He explains that with only a few bullets in those early days, they had to hit their mark quickly.

Joe's version today is a bit different. "I believe in fire, ready, aim." That's how he launched Spartan. There was no lengthy process.

Here's the answer to the street ban question I posed earlier in this chapter: The person who tried to stop me from talking was the *Interruptor*, and everyone else idly observing the press briefing were *Spectators*.

Of course there are people who would insist I was the *Interruptor*. They don't get it. That's why they have a long way to go to learn how to be an effective *Disruptor*. They are slaves to fake rules that don't really mean anything. I look at silly rules and say, "Give me a break!" They don't apply to me.

So who are you?

Disruptor?

Interruptor?

Spectator?

If you want to make things happen, is there any question which of the three you want to be?

RULES OF REINVENTION

DISRUPTORS RULE!

Disruptor

- Acts
- Innovates
- Has a thick skin
- Cuts through shit
- Goes against the flow
- Makes a difference (every day)
- Calls people on not delivering as promised
- Accepts some people will not like their style

Interruptor

- Reacts
- Gets in the way
- Is a contrarian
- Stalls, moves sideway or backward
- Feels threatened by others' progress and success
- Gets in the way for the sake of it

Spectator

- Spectates
- Doesn't take a stand
- Follows the leader
- Avoids risks

TRIBAL KNOWLEDGE
IS POWER

THROUGH THE YEARS I have been fortunate to work alongside people who were uniquely gifted. Their gift was not the mystical kind you read about with artists who have a vision or can't explain where their inspiration comes from.

The kind of gift I value most in the people I hire and work with is what I call *Tribal Knowledge*.

That's my phrase to describe workers who are so immersed in the nitty-gritty of their jobs that they have a sixth sense about what works and what doesn't. *Tribal Knowledge* is acquired through experience that is enhanced by a passion—an *Obsession* even—for being a *Master* at your job.

It's not about being flashy with fancy résumés of big, impressive-sounding names. That stuff doesn't particularly impress me. Not unless it's backed up by an all-in commitment.

I'm talking about people who are disciplined in learning their craft. I'm talking about people willing to sweat it out to continually improve their skill level. I'm talking about people who are totally prepared and ready to kill it when they get their big shot at stardom.

There are two types of stardom.

There's literal stardom, the one we associate with famous names who entertain us.

There's also business stardom. That is how I think of people in my universe whose names you wouldn't know but who I consider stars in their own right for what they contribute to their colleagues and to their company. Their gift—to themselves and to others—is *Tribal Knowledge*.

How *Tribal Knowledge* can pay back those who work hard at it is evident in what happened to Broadway musical ensemble member *Kathy Voytko*.

In December 2021 she was in the cast of *The Music Man*, starring **Hugh Jackman**, as a "swing." That is someone trained to step in to any one of several roles in a show if the principal performer cannot go on. Most of the swing roles are fairly small, with not many lines to memorize.

> Tribal Knowledge is acquired through experience that is enhanced by a passion—an Obsession even—for being a Master at your job.

READY FOR HER CLOSE-UP

On Christmas Eve it was fate that stepped in as *The Music Man*'s leading lady, **Sutton**

Foster, tested positive for COVID-19 and was not able to perform that night.

Voytko, who was a swing for eight different roles in the show, was notified at noon that day that she'd be playing opposite Jackman in the iconic role of Marian the Librarian. By 1:00 p.m., she was in full rehearsal mode, preparing to go on as Marian a few hours later.

Hugh Jackman onstage with Kathy Voytko.

At curtain call Hugh Jackman made a two-minute speech to the audience in praise of Voytko while also giving props to other swings in the cast.

"This is a time we've never known," said the film and stage superstar. He added, "We're in our fourth preview, so swings and understudies have not had a chance to learn. They get to watch and write notes as we rehearse over and over again. It humbles me … the courage, the brilliance, the dedication, the talent. The swings, the understudies, they are the bedrock of Broadway."

What Jackman said is as good a definition of *Tribal Knowledge* as any I've heard, with emphasis on "dedication." Voytko was not a pedigree performer in name, but she promised herself she would work hard to acquire the *Tribal Knowledge* necessary to be ready when her time came.

Even though Voytko's sudden star turn sounds like the script of a Hollywood movie, that kind of unexpected opportunity applies to any profession.

Consider basketball player *Caleb Martin* of the Miami Heat, one of the National Basketball Association's elite teams.

During the pandemic, the NBA made allowances for players who were stricken by the virus with ten-day hardship contracts to temporarily activate players not currently in the league. A lot of non-playing hoopsters lived out a fairy tale by getting phone calls out of nowhere asking them to suit up for an NBA team.

They put themselves in that position by staying in professional-caliber playing shape and not giving up the dream of one day making it to center court. You just never know when that one big break will break through for you. But you know you'd best be ready.

SCORING POINTS IN THE CLUTCH

Martin started the 2021–2022 season as the last player on the squad, but he made the most of his time on the floor by averaging a superb fifteen points a game while substituting for Heat star Jimmy Butler.

Heat Coach *Erik Spoelstra* called Martin "a can of Red Bull. He does everything intense."

One of the things I admire about the Heat, who I've been following closely for decades, is how their organization is built on *Tribal Knowledge*.

Heat president **Pat Riley**, a Hall of Fame coach and before that a player, has mentored players and coaches in Miami for nearly thirty years. Along with Riley is the strong leadership of head coach **Erik Spoelstra** and twenty-year veteran **Udonis Haslem**.

The Heat's **Tribal Knowledge** extends to how generous veterans are in spending time to mentor younger players. As a result the organization from the top down is looked up to as having the most dynamic and committed team culture in the league.

Once you're indoctrinated in the discipline and camaraderie of the Heat organization, it sticks with you for life. Even the presence of past Heat stars and game changers **LeBron James** and **Dwyane Wade** is felt to this day inside that locker room. An enduring legacy like that tells you that when it's used in the right way, **Tribal Knowledge** is power. Do you *want* that kind of power?

One of the core values of **Tribal Knowledge** is that it is not about one person. It's about people connecting with and helping each other in a common purpose. I put it like this: Companies with a good business plan and mediocre people don't make it. Companies with a good business plan and good people do.

KNOWLEDGE IS POWER

One of the superpowers of **Tribal Knowledge** is that it makes everyone successful who has it and who work together in good faith for the benefit of all, not just themselves.

Can you size up others fairly quickly, looking past their outward behavior to understand their true intentions? If you don't have that superpower now, you owe it to yourself to develop it.

Do you detect that a new coworker, for example, may have a hidden agenda that could get in the way of their colleagues or undermine the company business? Are they primarily out for themselves and will throw you or others under the bus to get ahead on their own terms? You have to stay aware of who is around you and what they are like. Don't waste time with people who play games.

Think of *Tribal Knowledge* as a set of tools that can be used to fix or build almost anything or to see new opportunities that are not obvious to others. It is knowledge that accrues from basic experience and the lessons of trial and error. Strong leaders understand people and how to get the most out of them. It's not about bossing people around. It's about being a people boss.

Tribal Knowledge is about using your wits and curiosity to explore situations. Just as I've employed people I knew I could rely on to get the job done right, throughout my career I've employed *Tribal Knowledge* to guide me in making the best decisions for all concerned.

What about having confidence in yourself and your persona? Be honest with yourself assessing that. I know who I am and make no excuses for how I am. You should do the same if you are making progress in life and career and treating people right.

Own your happiness and success. Don't apologize for it. It doesn't mean we all don't make mistakes. It means we own up to them. Don't dwell on something you might have done wrong or could have done better. Commit to yourself that you will get it right next time—and swiftly move on.

Tribal Knowledge doesn't overvalue surface effect. A pedigree isn't a free pass. I think of it primarily as optics, prone to emphasizing style and appearances over substance. Give me someone with grit over glamour every time. What a pedigree tends to look past is the same thing overlooked when someone stereotypes *Millennials* or any generation: *Individualism*. Each of us is unique, not a replica of each other.

DON'T LET PEDIGREES FOOL YOU

Where pedigrees are valuable and impressive in theory, if not always in practice, *Tribal Knowledge* is the practical application of our individual assets, what each of us brings to the table. *Tribal Knowledge* is not necessarily the absence of pedigree, but it doesn't rely on it to get the job done. It relies on hard work and ingenuity. It appreciates intangibles—reading between the lines to discover quality information you can't also find in raw numbers.

During the peak of the pandemic, it was painfully apparent to me (and I'm guessing to you as well) that the shortage of experienced and engaged sales people came at the cost of adequate customer service. I wrote a blog about it, aptly titled "The Help Needs Help." (You can read it at *MillennialBabyBoomer.com*.)

It was clear the newly hired workers standing behind counters were not armed with *Tribal Knowledge*, either about whatever they were selling, products or about how to properly work with customers.

I had one clerk suggest that I go to a competitor to answer my question because he had no clue what to do about it. That was a complete and unacceptable absence of *Knowledge*.

With some store staff, pandemic or not, you get the feeling they are not *Listening* to you. Weaponizing *Listening* is extremely important. It's all too easy to become distracted and lose focus, whether you're behind a counter or at the top of an organization.

Don't stop yourself from going further because you stopped paying close attention to the people you're serving—it can be a customer or an employee or a coworker.

I'm concerned about *Tribal Knowledge* turning into an endangered species these days. Retail, the business I've spent my life in, is not the same. I see it in different areas. Not many involved in retailing and manufacturing go by their instincts. Are they spending time in stores to find out what customers are thinking?

I realize the pandemic changed everyone's travel plans, to some extent perhaps permanently. But a major part of my *Tribal Knowledge* over the years was gained by going into stores and asking customers and salespeople what they want.

I miss the glamour that has faded in recent years from the fashion industry. The jobs are too much a mechanical process. The positive power that emotion brings to making business fun and more productive is hard to find now.

That vibe comes from trusting your instincts and being passionate about creating excitement and freshness in whatever you do, whether it's retail or accounting or insurance. You should be *Obsessed* with your product to ensure it meets, or exceeds, customer expectations.

ALL IN ON MENTORING

I make it a priority to *Mentor* graduate students in Fashion Design and Fashion Management at *FIT* for a very simple reason: I know from experience how important being *Mentored* is to succeed in the real world. I go all in on mentoring to help the students in as many ways as possible. Take your *Tribal Knowledge* and share it with the world!

I learned a lasting lesson about the importance of *Listening* to them when I decided to change the music they heard when shopping in *rue21* stores. We had been playing Top 40 tunes. But I was fascinated by the techno sounds I heard when checking out *Abercrombie & Fitch*. So we switched to that kind of soundtrack.

The result? The only ones who hated the new music more than our customers were our store associates. They told us customers liked to sing and dance to the music when shopping and couldn't do that with the techno tracks. I made a mistake with that decision by ignoring the *Tribal Knowledge* of our customers and even my own *Tribal Knowledge* since the Top 40 music was so popular there was no good reason to change it. So we immediately changed it back.

I use stories like that to give guidance on how to relate to customers. What made *rue21* successful overall was *Tribal Knowledge*, not of what we wanted but of what our customers wanted.

A word of warning about *Tribal Knowledge*: It can be an illusion or, more to the point, a delusion. I'm talking especially about social media. Much of it is the opposite of *Tribal Knowledge*. It's people posing as somebody else or aspiring to be something that's unrealistic or sloganeering. There's a serious shortage of authentic sentiment on social media.

I'm much less interested in influencing social media than I am in influencing real life. There's a difference. You can influence people by what you stand up to believe. You have to be in the pulse of the moment. You must have conviction.

CONNECT AND PROSPER

You can collect *Tribal Knowledge* through connections that you make. There are times I'll encourage someone I am *Mentoring* to use me as a reference with a decision-maker who is in a position to help them either get a job or network with other business influencers.

Very often it *does* come down to who you know. Like it or not, that's just how the world works. The wider your circle of influencers who can help you, the wider and deeper your *Tribal Knowledge* of the field you want to work in. In addition to *Tribal Knowledge*, having the right connections is powerful.

Tribal Knowledge is not a tool I used only in my business dealings. It extends to my personal life as well. When I like a certain restaurant and become a regular patron, I make it a point to get to know the maître d' or the owner and what they are about. That makes a noticeable difference in how you are treated when you dine there. The same personal connection works when shopping in a boutique store or when I'm traveling.

I talked about Caleb Martin and Kathy Voytko earlier in this chapter as high-profile examples of succeeding because of *Tribal Knowledge*. It doesn't matter who you are, though. Even if your performance space is an office cubicle instead of a basketball court or a Broadway stage, you should be preparing for a possible star turn by practicing *Tribal Knowledge*.

The wider your circle of influencers who can help you, the wider and deeper your *Tribal Knowledge* of the field you want to work in.

People in the business world can benefit from working as hard as possible every day, without a spotlight on them, and still find ways to shine when the moment comes for their close-up. *MAB* member *Rick Hartmann*, who works for a reinsurance broker, personifies the kind of no-nonsense worker who knows you don't need to be flamboyant to stand out. In fact, he was smart enough during the pandemic to stand out by doing the same thing he had been doing up to that point—simply going to the office.

Rick says working from the office offered him such key benefits as "collegiality, camaraderie, exposure to senior business leaders, and the opportunity for **Mentoring**." At the height of the pandemic, he says 90 percent of the two-hundred-person office simply didn't show up, at least not in person.

Being one of the handful of people who sucked it up and continued going to the office enabled Rick to bond with one of his company's presidents. "Normally, you're competing for their time and attention," Rick says, "but when almost nobody is going in, you have the opportunity for conversations about your job and your career."

The result? When a senior VP slot opened, Rick was tapped to fill it. When the president and CEO award was handed out, Rick was on the receiving end, two years in a row.

A WEALTH OF HUMILITY

Merrill wealth manager Jeff Erdmann has a great perspective on *Tribal Knowledge* and how it has helped him persevere and prevail as the perennial number one practitioner in his field. He actually credits dyslexia, a condition that makes letters and words appear jumbled to the eyes.

Jeff Erdmann with Bob

Jeff says as a result of his dealing with dyslexia, "For thirty years, I thought others were smarter than me." Yet he turned that seeming disability into what he calls a gift because he says, "It made me humble. I don't know any successful person who isn't humble."

Humility is a huge part of *Tribal Knowledge*. Know what you don't know. Treat other people kindly. "What is most important for young people to learn to be successful is likability," says Jeff.

I know firsthand Jeff exudes that enviable quality himself, and it has served him exceptionally well in life and career.

Do you make it a point to be nice to others? Do you want to be liked? That's all part of the *Tribal Knowledge* mix.

Remember the tale of Kathy Voytko, who didn't squander the knowledge that all swings, like her, must be prepared at all times for their big break—whenever it comes.

As Hugh Jackman told that Christmas Eve 2021 *The Music Man* audience, which went wild with appreciation when he revealed that Voytko was given only five hours to get ready to star in a Broadway smash hit and made the most of it, "Take it from me, the real superheroes do not wear capes."

Because, after all, the show *must* go on. When you get the call, are you ready to show up with your *Tribal Knowledge* to become a star?

RULES OF REINVENTION

ARE YOU FOR REAL?

Using **Tribal Knowledge** to your best advantage—in your career and your life—means you first must master key traits about yourself. Some of what I describe below already may be part of you. Other qualities may prove more challenging. That's okay. Nothing worthwhile comes without a great deal of **Effort**.

Check out this list to discover what it takes to be a **Tribal Knowledge Warrior**, then get to work filling in the gaps you identify as missing or inadequate in yourself.

- Are you **Authentic** and **Empathetic** enough? That means you tell it like it is and don't play mind games with people. You are honest and humble. You care about the welfare of others. You don't waste time with BS.

- Do you **Admit and Learn from Mistakes**? Nobody expects you to have all the answers all the time. So don't act like you do!

- Do you **Collaborate** well with others? **Tribal Knowledge** is a team sport. Give credit to others for good ideas and help them build on those ideas.

- How **Consistent** and **Persistent** are you? These go hand in hand and are often overlooked parts of being **Successful**. Don't give up because you tried something and failed. We learn more from failure than from **Success**.

- Is your **Work Ethic** strong enough? It can never be *too* strong, but it can be too weak. It helps tremendously if you enjoy what you do. If you don't, then work harder at finding your **Calling**.

- Are you comfortable in your **Confidence**? If you wish you had more, look inside yourself to see where you come up short, then **Commit** yourself to closing the gap day by day.

SUCCESS IS FOR THE BRAVE!

A YOUNG WOMAN I MENTOR had a *Fear* of heights. So she climbed a seventy-four-foot tree to overcome that phobia.

She also had a thing about putting her feet in muddy waters. So naturally, like anybody would in that situation, she took herself to the Amazon (the one with water) and stuck her legs in the muck to get over that *Fear*.

What does any of that have to do with ***Fear of Success***? A lot. Yes, the phrase ***Fear of Success*** can sound strikingly similar to Fear of Failure, even though Success is the opposite of Failure.

We don't always realize we are afraid of success. Sometimes people stop themselves because of that fear. Having ***Fear of Success*** is a gift. It's the *Fear* that propels you to ***Succeed***. As corny as it sounds, that kind of *Fear* is your friend.

In my *Mentee*'s case, she wasn't afraid of failing at something she was expected to do—or that she needed to do. I don't know of many bosses who would direct an employee to climb a tall tree or wade into muddy waters.

Instead, she set personal goals for herself that tested her limits, and that expanded her skill set, and that pushed her to taste the delicious flavor of *Success*. The *Fear* of achievement—of doubting yourself—is what makes the pinnacle of *Success* so precious. If it comes too easy, how special can it be?

Anyone intent on building a memorable career must explore how to eliminate *Fear of Success*. When all is said and done, although it lasts, *Fear of Success* is not at all a bad sensation. It means you're ambitious. It is a by-product of the power of passion. It's okay to constantly have that *Fear* challenged. That's how you cope with it, if not eliminate it altogether.

People who have a *Success* mode think about what they can do to sustain the feeling of being *Fearless* and strong in overcoming obstacles. In my personal and professional lives, I come across a wide variety of people. Different ages, backgrounds, lifestyles, tastes. One thing they have in common, though, is *Fear*. Not the same *Fear*. It might be *Fear of Success*, *Fear* of failure, *Fear* of others, even *Fear* of themselves.

It could be someone telling me about a date they went on. It went very well, they say. And yet they also say they *Fear* not having handled it well. There's no reason for them to feel that way. At least no reason they can explain. You may call that kind of *Fear* irrational, but that's beside the point. The point is they are feeling it. So rational or not, the *Fear* is real to them. That's all that matters.

My advice to that person is simple: "Stop worrying. Just be yourself." That's my advice to you too and to everyone. File that advice under *Confidence*.

IGNORE NAYSAYERS

I never worried about competition or people who were out to get me. Those are very real factors in *Fear of Success*. Do you have the stomach to deal with competitors who may even play dirty? Are you willing to manage the stress that comes from naysayers and doubters and even those who may lie about you?

They were there for me too, make no mistake. But I did two things to deal with it: I showed people by my actions what I was capable of accomplishing. That's one. The other way I manage those situations is to push back harder than the person trying to push my buttons.

One of those people was an executive who told me outright he wouldn't support a new business plan I was presenting to our corporate leaders. He went so far as to suggest the only way I would succeed in my plan would be over his dead body. I came right back at him and said if that's how he feels, he should be ready to assume that position because I was determined to succeed.

He had *Fear of Success*, all right. He *Feared my Success*! By the way, that guy I went to war with happened to be my boss on the org chart, but it wasn't long before he was gone from the chart and the company.

To say he had a bad attitude is an understatement. You'll come across people like that in your career and your life. If you're not ready to dig in your heels and *Take a Stand*, as I did, you have nobody to blame but yourself. The more someone like that doesn't respect you, the more you should respect yourself even more by conquering your *Fears* and not letting them get in your way.

When someone mistreats me without justification, I get back at them but not by being vindictive because that's just playing their silly game. Instead, their slighting me stokes the fire in my stomach to be *Successful* by showing results.

Do you know who else *Fears* someone else's *Success*? Men, that's who. A lot of them *Fear* female *Success*. As I pointed out in my first book, *Fisch Tales*, that kind of male is easily threatened by a level playing field with the opposite sex. The familiar phrase "glass ceiling" illustrates the suppression of female executives in the business world, a prejudice that exists for no reason other than they are not male.

In the companies I've run, I was gender-blind. I regarded and treated people purely on their contributions to our business and on their professional attitude. For a leader or manager to think any other way is self-sabotage. You're placing your own biases—based on gender—ahead of what's good for business. I also wasn't very tolerant when men who worked for me treated females in the company as somehow lesser in ability than male employees. I was clear and concise about my advice: deal with it!

They probably cursed me behind my back for that, but I could not care less. I can't emphasize enough that you simply cannot be bothered by what people think about you when you are taking a stand.

I know it's easy for me to say because I never have worried about that kind of blowback, but if you do care, to the point of distraction, it's time to stop. Nobody has control over you except you.

I am not telling you to ignore those who want to help you and have the tools and experience to do that. That's where *Mentors* enter the picture. It's important to pick your *Mentors* carefully.

A worthwhile *Mentor* will help you identify and develop what you are good at. They will help you manage your *Fear of Success*. You'd be surprised who can act as a *Mentor* when you most need help in a specific area or task. It doesn't even need to be an adult.

DANCING WITH SADIE ROBERTSON

At *rue21*, we worked with TV personality and motivational influencer *Sadie Robertson* as our spokesperson. Apart from being part of TV's popular *Duck Dynasty* family of reality TV stars, Sadie is an extremely successful young woman on her own with millions of followers on social media. I can tell you from my personal experience that she is as genuine and soulful as they come.

Stephanie, Bob, and Sadie

When Sadie was sixteen, popular TV series *Dancing with the Stars* invited her to be a contestant. Makes sense. TV is all about ratings, and the producers look for big names who will attract new viewers to the show.

Except there was one small problem: Sadie said she was scared. She was not confident in her dancing enough to go in front of millions of viewers. She didn't think she was good enough.

Then someone intervened to serve as a kind of mentor: Sadie's younger sister *Bella*, who was eleven at the time.

Bella went to work, reminding Sadie how she always would preach about standing for what you believe and be *Fearless*.

Bella tapped into the **Confidence** she knew Sadie has in many other ways and convinced her sister that she would be great, that it would be a fun experience, that it would only add to her **Confidence** and make her a better dancer than she already was. And **Succeed** Sadie did. She placed second in the competition! She realized she could be successful with anything she put her mind to. I'd call that realization a major personal **Success** in itself, wouldn't you?

If you're thinking that's **Fear of Failure**, not **Fear of Success**, think about this: A show like that is not based on failing, like one of those survivor-theme shows. It's based on giving your best performance. Another important difference is that on *Dancing with the Stars*, the star, in this case Sadie, is paired with a professional dancer who trains the celebrity to dance like a star!

In other words, Sadie was aware her **Mentor** and trainer would be a world-class dancer whose job it is to help her **Succeed**. Yet she still could not bring herself to take advantage of that golden opportunity and impress people on national television.

If you are afraid to take the risk of being **Successful**, you'll never **Succeed** because life is about taking **Risks**. So **Fear of Success**, in that sense, is rational and should be embraced. You know it's a **Risk** and are apprehensive about it. So it's a different form of **Fear**.

> **If you are afraid to take the risk of being *Successful*, you'll never *Succeed* because life is about taking *Risks*.**

We hear about sibling rivalry. I think that's a great example of sibling support. Sadie's insecurity about going on the show was conquered with the help of her sister.

146

Essentially, Bella was telling Sadie to just be herself, to go out and use her natural talents in a new way—on a dance floor, in front of a national TV audience. The lesson there is to be yourself where you can achieve the things in life you want to do. You have to live with yourself your whole life.

I tell people they shouldn't waste time doing something that they have no *Confidence* they can do. Instead, go after what you think you can do and make something happen with it.

ARE YOU A BELIEVER?

I *Mentor* and advise people to think for themselves to get ahead. Your *Opportunities* are endless. You have to believe that, not because I say so but because you value your self-esteem. If you believe you can do whatever you want, you will be *Successful*. I only want to work with people who really want to do something with themselves.

The kind of *Insecurity* Sadie was experiencing, even if momentary, is a big factor in *Fear of Success*. *Fear* freezes people. It helps visualize being *Fearless*. Imagine what it looks like. What characteristics make you *Fearless*? If you've heard the famous expression "fake it till you make it," then how about applying that to acting *Fearless*? If you do that, you're halfway home.

Do you have a mantra that you live by? I have multiple mantras. One of them is *Whatever It Takes*. That's about sticking to your *Values*, following your gut instincts, and not being discouraged. We are all capable of more than we think. You need to put your mind to it and be obsessively *Passionate* about fulfilling your *Aspirations*.

Another mantra is *The Sky Is the Limit*. There are people who have decent careers but don't go as far as they envision and talk about. It makes me wonder if they really want to achieve to the max their

Dreams and *Goals*, or do they just say they do? How badly do they really want it? Are they willing to change to get what they want? Or do they just want it to be their way? Do you bend the world to your will or adapt yourself to the world?

There are two ways to deal with *Fear of Success*: You let it stop you or slow you down. That's one way. The other way is you ride it like you're taming a wild horse. You harness it as energy and motivation. You use it to fuel your *Obsession*.

During one of the monthly salons I host with our *MAB*, our guest speaker *Megan Rose Johnson* shared a lesson on fear. She spoke of various *Fears*: *Fear* of not being good enough, *Fear* of failing, *Fear* of being vulnerable. What, she asked, if we stop letting *Fear* take control? What if you reflect on these limiting beliefs about yourself? Change the narrative of the *Fear* to be your fuel to take action. Remember, daily steps amounts to 365 steps. Megan is an inspiration!

One of the common symptoms of *Fear of Success* is the mistaken—and even at times dangerous—idea that you need to *Stay in Your Lane*. You know who says that? Insecure bosses and colleagues who *Fear* their own inadequacies and have little faith in their own efforts at *Success*. Or maybe you just say that to yourself, which I would tell you is even worse. If nobody else is trying to hold you back with the phony *Stay in Your Lane* advice, why are you telling yourself to do that? *Fear of Success.* That's why.

Staying in Your Lane is the fast lane to going nowhere special. The lane is your comfort zone. Had I done that, I'd have a very nice career as a middle manager in a sprawling retail organization where I would be part of the pack.

But I'm not a great role model when it comes to *Fear of Success* because I'm not built that way. Some people who knew me or worked with me along the way might tell you, if anything, that maybe if I had

Fear of Success, it would have tempered my *Obsessive* style, slowed me down. And they'd be right. Which is why I am glad I didn't have that kind of *Fear*. At the same time, I empathize with those who do, which is why I wanted to give the subject its own chapter.

Maybe I didn't experience *Fear of Success* because, when it came to key decisions, I wasn't afraid to *Put It on the Line*. I might have been anxious about making it happen, but I wasn't afraid of being *Successful*.

FREEDOM AND INDEPENDENCE

Starting with my very first job, I had no fear that I could be *Successful*. I felt *Liberated* that I didn't have to rely on my parents to make a life for myself. That was a great day. It just carried with me for the rest of my life. My motivation was *Freedom* and *Independence*. I never worried about how much money I was going to make. My assumption was that if I work hard—doing something I greatly enjoyed so it didn't feel like work—the rewards would come eventually. And they did.

I am living proof that "there is no greater liberty than to work for your freedom." That statement was made by *The Unstoppables'* Bill Wooditch when he interviewed me on his excellent podcast.

Making mistakes and taking *Risks* serve a purpose. I've had a very rewarding career doing just that every step of the way. Did I make mistakes? Who doesn't! But training yourself to rebound from your mistakes is a form of self-improvement. It's a good way to develop *Fortitude* in the face of adverse circumstances.

Let's talk about the benefits of *Obsession* for a minute too. My advice is pure and simple: If you're not *Obsessed*, then you don't really want *Success*. If you really want it, you need to be *Obsessed*.

When you say you are going to do something and make it happen, guess what. You better make it happen. Too many fall down because they promise things and fail to deliver. A lot of people I've encountered have great ideas and promise, but it ends there. They don't deliver. I even will check backgrounds to see if they have delivered before.

As *FIT*'s Brooke Carlson put it, "I like the concept of having a high say-to-do ratio. People remember a lot what you say and commit to. Be *Honest* and be your best, and keep your word when making a *Commitment*."

It's common (and logical) that people who have *Fear of Success* don't have something that would help lessen it: a plan. I like to call it a *Vision*. When you run your life without a plan or *Vision*, you could lose sight of your destination, stumble, and hurt yourself. You slow yourself down and lose ground instead of progressing toward your *Goal*. People without a direction will rationalize why that is, and they know they are rationalizing. It becomes a vicious circle that leads them nowhere—or nowhere special.

Another cause of *Fear of Success* is being empathetic to a fault. As you'll read elsewhere in this book, I place great value on the human quality of *Empathy*. What I'm saying here is that it can be misplaced. What do I mean by that? There are times *Empathy* is not called for, particularly when it is used as an excuse for holding yourself back.

FOLLOW YOUR AMBITION

Consider the case of *Jenny Byrom Betzler*, an assistant buyer who worked for me at *rue21*. *Jenny B.*, as I called her, wanted to be promoted to buyer. Great! I love *Ambition*. You might even say, as a

Mentor and motivational author and speaker, that *Ambitious* people are my business.

There was a hitch in Jenny B.'s *Ambition*, though. She *Feared* that her strong desire to upgrade her position and advance her career would somehow offend her colleagues. Enter *Fear of Success*. Not so great! "Then you'll never be a buyer," I advised her. I'm glad to say she realized her *Fears* were unfounded and became an excellent buyer.

As you work your way toward whatever goals you have set up for yourself, be mindful not to overanalyze your *Progress*. Keep track of the *Progress*, of course. But don't get caught up in the so-called analysis paralysis. *Ambition* is characterized by *Passion* more than it is by analytics. There are times in your journey to fruition that *Go with Your Gut* is better "technical" advice than relying on the metrics of a data-dense spreadsheet.

Fear of Success can manifest itself through indecision.

Sports legends *Tiger Woods* and LeBron James, marketing legend Steve Jobs, and music legend Bruce Springsteen are singular examples of how far huge *Ambition* can take you—if you don't get in its way. But rather than paralyzing their *Progress* by overanalyzing how to get there, they sucked it up big time and fought their way to *Greatness*. *Fear of Success* can manifest itself through indecision, which none of those three suffered from. Each was supremely *Confident* in their abilities to be the best in their field and *Succeed* where others had not.

In our podcast conversation, *The Unstoppables'* Bill Wooditch emphasized that, to *Succeed*, "You have to think and do." He called the two key ingredients "*Common Sense* and *Urgency*." Without those two, numbers are irrelevant. "So many of us are caught in the crosshairs of indecision." My version of what he's talking about is to tell people to *Not Confuse Issues with Logic*. That's what causes analysis paralysis and indecision. What we think of as logical in theory doesn't always make sense in real life.

That reminds me to remind you that, in this book and in *Fisch Tales*, every story I tell and every lesson I share is not based on theory. It's what I have directly experienced in life and business.

Fear of Success also can come from not wanting more responsibilities, with being content in your own world, where you are not responsible for anyone but yourself. *Fear of Success* can come from not wanting to be "the bad guy," for example, being the boss who has to show tough love and fire people and not always be the nicest person in the room. Some people simply are afraid of being in the limelight.

WEAK LEADERS

Bill Wooditch made a great point about that, saying that it's a weak leader who needs to be liked. They also risk being easily manipulated by people in a way that's not helpful to anybody except the manipulator.

Conversely, as Bill also pointed out, there are weak leaders who lead through *Fear* by trying to manipulate people. As he said, "At the end of the day, you're left with your ego in a room." And that is a cold and lonely place to be.

If you are too *Timid* to accept that with *Success* at work, and a steady rise to increased *Responsibility*, comes the need to have a tough skin and not be universally liked by those you manage, then you are too *Timid* to benefit from this book.

Speaking of a tough skin, I had the privilege of working for one very tough dude by the name of *Leonardo Del Vecchio*. He was chairman and CEO of *Luxottica*, a powerful global conglomerate, and one of the richest people in the world. Once, when I made the mistake of *Fearlessly* asking him for what I felt was a more impressive and appropriate title, he turned on me for a moment and shouted, in total sarcasm, "I make you emperor!" That was his way of saying to me "Are you serious? That's what you're concerned about?" He didn't scare me away. That episode simply reminded me to pick my battles carefully.

Success also comes to those who overcome their *Fear* of making mistakes. As Bill said, it's good to fail if you fail with the intent to *Improve*.

If you are afraid to take the risk of being *Successful*, you'll never *Succeed*. Because life is about taking *Risks*. So *Fear of Success*, in that sense, is rational and should be embraced. You know it's a risk and are apprehensive about it. So it's a different form of *Fear*.

The more you take charge to eliminate *Fear of Success* by pushing yourself, the more *Success* you'll know.

When you are *Fearless*, it's a great feeling, as if you are master of the universe, at least of your universe, and that's good enough.

The only way to manage the *Fear of Success* is to go for the gold. *Put It on the Line.* People tend to not be so much afraid of *Success*, as they are apprehensive about all the hard work it takes to get there.

Fear of Success doesn't mean you don't want to *Succeed*. It means you do but have anxiety about getting there. That's perfectly normal. The thought to activate is transforming anxiety about yourself and your *Ambitions* into belief in yourself and your *Ambitions*.

You are testing that transformation with *Fear of Success*. That's more than okay. It means you are thinking about it. It means it is top of mind. You're on the right track.

It's good to fail if you fail with the intent to *Improve*.

RULES OF REINVENTION

BEING A PROFESSIONAL VICTIM SUCKS!

- Whenever I hear someone whine to me about being pigeon-holed in their job, I turn that right around on them. I tell them, "Wrong! Nobody's pigeonholing you. You're pigeon-holing yourself!"

- The problem is it's all too easy to put yourself in that position. I call it being a **Professional Victim**. It happens when you're afraid to speak up for yourself. That's on you, so don't go finger-pointing and playing the blame game.

- We need to feel as if we make a difference. It could be on the job. It could be at home with a spouse or kids. There are times to lean back, and there are times to take the lead so that others follow you. Let them be pigeonholed, not you! We should be in control of what we do. If you let others control you, shame on *you*, not them.

- Here are some tips on how *not* to be a **Professional Victim**—or a pigeon.

- Be **Fearless**. Visualize it. What does it look like? It means **Speak Up!** when you have something strong to say, even if it means disagreeing with your boss. Acting **Fearless** makes you **Fearless**!

- Be **Confident** in your overall ability to complete small tasks and to realize your dream. Insecurity is a major contributor to **Fear of Success**. Do whatever it takes to not let it defeat you.

- Be **Obsessed**. I'm not telling you to go crazy in an undisciplined, scattershot way. Focus your **Obsession** wisely, and don't let others deter you from your **Vision** and what you know you are capable of **Achieving**.

BACK TO THE FUTURE (A.K.A. "THE FEEL")

THE METAVERSE IS SEXY. Dangerously sexy. The whole idea of it is to surround us in artificial reality, a triumph of technology.

Ask yourself, though, if it is wise to surrender ourselves to tech and leave it at that, or should we control technology and fit it into our **Authentic** reality? If you are okay with surrendering yourself to technology—or to anything else—bye-bye, thanks for making it this far, but this book is not for you. You're too timid to go out and *Get a Life*!

I don't serve technology. It serves my needs as I see fit. Humans rule, not machines. If we let them take the lead in our lives, either consciously or by inaction, they eventually *will* rule.

As our culture continues to mechanize through fast-advancing technology, we've got to keep our grip on controlling our own destiny. One of the best things about Zoom becoming our meeting place during the pandemic is that it made us appreciate the beauty and value of physical connection. That's how we should view technology—as a support system for humans, not a replacement for humans.

To keep ourselves and each other in the pulse of what it means to be human and remind ourselves the many ways we are irreplaceable by machines, we all need to study **Humanology 101**.

"The more things change, the more they stay the same."

The more I hear that, the more I wonder how true it is these days.

Things constantly are changing. No question about that. We live in a time of unimaginable human progress, with a capital *P*.

There's a lot of capital influencing our world today. Corporate capital keeps growing exponentially, with companies like Apple worth trillions. Apple's—and Google's and Amazon's—intellectual capital in turn creates technological capital, like *AI*.

All of that capital is propelling human evolution at warp speed. By 2030 it's projected that 90 percent of the world's population will be online.

Once upon a time, entertainment like *Star Wars* imagined the future as science fiction. With space travel for civilians no longer a far-off fantasy, it's fair to say the future has arrived, with a capital *F*. As we futurize everything about our daily existence—at work, at home, at play—there is one capital I'm worried about: **Human Capital**.

That's **Back to the Future**.

WHAT IS "THE FEEL"?

It's a major theme of my *FIT* Fireside Chats. There's a convenient metaphor I use when speaking with students so I can make tangible for them the intangible idea of human capital: I describe the importance of *The Feel* of merchandise in apparel retailing.

Whether it's a fabric designer, a picker, a merchant, or a customer, pivotal decisions on what is sellable and what is not are made based, in part, on how a fabric feels to a *human hand*. To be clear, it's not just the color, or the name of the material, or the design. They all matter, but how it *Feels* often is the secret sauce that can make or break a garment.

Maybe one day, long after we're gone, machine learning will replicate that tactile sensation of the all-important *Feel*, but I don't see that happening in our lifetimes.

The same uniquely human factor of *Feel* applies not just in apparel retailing but also everywhere, and it's being challenged by the onslaught of unfeeling technology.

To be clear, I'm bullish about using technology such as data analytics as much as possible to improve our businesses, our economy, our lives, our future. I'm definitely down with all of that. If I were running a retailer today, I'd be all over the data. You use the best information you can find to optimize your strategy. As I look back on my fifteen years at *rue21*, knowing what I know now, I admit that there are areas of data science I would have handled differently.

Yet like other forms of *Progress*, we also need to not let ourselves be overwhelmed by data science to the point that it controls us. Instead, we should be harnessing it to *optimize* the decision-making process.

We need to push back just enough to exert our dominance over technology. There are all kinds of doomsday scenarios—not limited to science fiction anymore—where robots replace humans in certain types of jobs when repetitive behavior and data processing (like accounting) is required.

To future-proof yourself and your skills, you must differentiate yourself and the *Value* you add to whomever pays you, even if you're self-employed. A machine can crunch numbers and do it faster, better, and cheaper. Anybody can whip up a spreadsheet or PowerPoint and dazzle a boardroom of senior management.

But that is just the point: just about anybody can do that, so what is the unique human value that you bring to the table?

How do you use your specialness to improve your performance, to improve your company's performance, and to make sure your boss knows about it?

The *FIT* graduate students have heard me tell them *never* to forget who is the most important person in any business. It's not the CEO. It's the *Customer*! A common stumble made by business people is to consider their reaction or their *Feel* for a product without stopping to consider what the *Customer* feels about that same product. Isn't that much more important than what you think? How does what you're doing fit with what your target *Customer* is doing?

That's *Back to the Future*.

DISCOVER YOURSELF

There's another big point I make to the *FIT* students: It's a shame if you're talented but don't let the people who can help you see that talent. It is possible to hide behind technology as a kind of crutch. Some people need to be pushed to show the world why they are special.

They also need to push themselves, to form strong beliefs about what they're doing and make those beliefs known to the people who can help them grow. You've got to do that yourself to take your talent to fruition and get ahead. Don't count on being "discovered." This is real life, not Hollywood.

I look into a room of students and ask, out loud, to their faces, "Who are the next bright people who want to make something of themselves at whatever level?" When I was in a similar position—as an executive trainee in my first retailing job at A&S in the 1970s—I heard the head of the company say something similar in welcoming 125 of us to the company.

He was very specific in stating that only one of us—that is, under 1 percent of us—would climb the corporate ladder to upper management positions in the following decade. I decided right then and there that I would be the one. And I kept on schedule, every step of the way. Within thirteen years, I was President and CEO of apparel retailer *TH Mandy*.

My career has been helped by staying **Confident** and relying on **Gut Instinct**. Whenever I would visit *rue21* stores, I always made it a point to chat up the store manager and staff to make them feel super appreciated.

I treated them like stars because that's really how I felt about their critical role in our **Success**. Understanding how to use data is integral to meeting and surpassing business goals. That doesn't eliminate the equally valuable resource of **Human Capital**. A **Passion** of mine is respecting the principle that any positive outcome starts with the right people.

My "people first" philosophy stayed consistent on the corporate side of being CEO. I've never been interested in pursuing financial plays as a method to make money, for me or the company. I prefer to stay connected to and cultivate the human side of the company culture rather than get too caught up in the theatricality of financial plays. That's how I stay in the pulse of the business—through people.

That's **Back to the Future**.

Another strong piece of advice I always throw out there: don't listen to anyone—and I mean *anyone*—who says you need to **Stay in Your Lane**. Bullshit!

I tell students and others I mentor the opposite—do yourself a big favor and **Learn Other Lanes**. Whenever someone pulled that "lane" line on me, I'm not sure they ever heard me mutter, "Yeah. Fat chance!" but they found out soon enough by my actions that my **Lane** was wherever I decided I wanted it to be.

TAKE THIS LANE AND SHOVE IT

If the **Lane** losers try to bully you—out of jealousy or political infighting or for whatever lame reason—just smile patronizingly (they're asking for it, right?) and deploy their tight-ass advice as great **Motivation** to take a stand on your own behalf. For good measure, you might come right out and let them know, "Do what you want, but you don't need to 'splain **Lanes** to me."

Being **Bold** today is more necessary than ever, as data, AI, and the internet of things reshape our behavior and perspective. All bets were off during the pandemic, giving people permission to go for broke, quitting jobs, and in some cases, jumping into the gig economy. That entrepreneurial spirit needs to keep going and growing.

Protect your *Passion* and amplify it with technology to propel your destiny. That's a winning combination.

160

As I see it, the ascent of technology is daring us as humans to become more engaged and more committed in anything and everything we do. As fundamental as the real-life *Matrix* is to our lives (digital media, devices, apps), none of that has the secret power that you have: *Passion*. Protect your *Passion* and amplify it with technology to propel your destiny. That's a winning combination.

And that's *Back to the Future*.

During the height of the COVID-19 pandemic, I saw close-up what can happen when *Passion* is missing from the human equation. It felt as if everywhere I went, including stores where I am a familiar face, customer service was *out of service*. It's too easy to just blame it as the aftermath of the COVID-19 shutdown. The lack of *Passion* and engagement by retail personnel was already evident prepandemic.

I don't blame the person on the sales floor or behind the counter. The *Responsibility* is on management for not investing enough in any company's most valuable asset: its people. In the AI age of machine learning, there's been a shift in emphasis away from human learning and training.

You see it in shops where technical knowledge is taken for granted by customers, like a *Best Buy* or a *Verizon* store. Their expertise is the whole point of their value proposition, yet those places don't always hire the right people for the skill positions. Some on the selling floor unintentionally reveal that they don't know much more about what they're selling than the person who's buying it. These retailers have refocused so strongly on e-commerce they are staffing stores with poorly trained associates.

A Verizon store worker couldn't figure out how to perform a basic task on my Verizon phone … and then suggested I take it to Best Buy!

STRANGERS IN A STRANGE LAND

Those reliable resources of information behind the counter who knew and pampered their best customers suddenly were few and far between. Instead of feeling comfortable and welcome when out in the market, it can seem as if we're strangers in a strange land, with store associates impersonating robots whose resting face is a blank stare.

The same blank stare syndrome can be virtually "seen" when speaking on the phone with a customer service representative halfway across the world.

You see the malaise too in fast-food franchises, where it can take an inordinate length of time to pay for a simple order because the cashier is laboring over how to complete the transaction.

Without necessary training as a core commitment in a company's *Best Practices*, we are losing standards and enabling *Mediocrity* in the workforce.

The training crisis is not at all restricted to the retail sector.

A relative told me that feeling isolated in her office job led to an ironic *Epiphany*: by fending for herself, without any input from her supervisor, who also is not benefiting from job development, she realized that she was passing him in capability (if not in compensation, which becomes the impetus to leave for a better *Opportunity*).

Accountability always starts in the same place—at the top of the organization chart.

If you run a business, ask yourself, "Are we spending enough time training people once we hire them?"

If you work for someone, ask yourself, "Am I being trained constantly and adequately enough to do my job better and to serve the customer better?"

That *Empathetic* connection between people involved in a transaction is also a *Feel* that's gone missing in the office culture.

As amazing as Amazon and other online retailers are with customer service, and offering depth and breadth of inventory, I can't reach through the screen to feel the merchandise or try on athletic shoes.

Technology is great, but there are some things that can't be replaced, such as *Intuition* or physical contact with the *Feel* of a fabric. We'd be foolish not to take advantage of the scientific advances that optimize the customer experience, improve product quality, or create new businesses for entrepreneurs to capitalize on.

We'd also be foolish to inhabit a future that leaves behind *Best Practices* that are timeless and work to our advantage in any era.

That's *Back to the Future*.

AI = AUTHENTIC INTELLIGENCE

In the fashion industry, I'll hear people say, "We don't need designers. We have artificial intelligence (AI) and augmented reality (AR) to do that and do it faster and cheaper than human designers."

But who is it that designs AI and AR applications? It starts with real people. People with *Instincts* based on *Experience* and *Tribal Knowledge*.

Sure, with machine learning, a computer can try to predict, like Las Vegas oddsmakers, winners, and losers.

But it requires someone with *Tribal Knowledge* to look at that granular data and detect patterns or detect aberrations that only the professional can explain and then suggest corrective action.

Ana Jablinski was a second-year graduate student at *FIT* who I continue to mentor. She was concerned about what would be the perfect lace material for her dresses. She wanted them to be as captivating as possible to attract buyers. So she was motivated to sweat the details. She understands *The Feel*. That's as good an illustration as any of what I mean by *The Feel*. A machine is not going to worry about that. Only a human would know to do that.

That's **Back to the Future**.

Tribal Knowledge is authentic wisdom that accumulates over time. It is *not* replaceable solely by AI. Data is an invaluable tool in the decision-making process, but it needs **Human Capital** to extract meaning and analysis. That's what I mean by the title of this chapter—**Back to the Future**. The best way to make **Progress** is by remembering the **Best Practices** of our past. We are so used to saying that machines make us smarter we have forgotten that the reverse is just as true—people with **Tribal Knowledge** make machines look smarter too.

What do you do when you are building a business or a product line and don't have historical data to learn from? You do what I do: **Go with Your Gut**!

At **rue21**, my growth strategy was based on building product categories, including departments such as fragrance and beauty that didn't exist in our stores when I took over the company. For those new categories, we had this much data—zero!

But that didn't faze me. I knew we had a different form of research to draw on. It was not based on hard numbers but on anecdotal knowledge, courtesy of **rue21**'s **Teen Board**. It was the strong recommendation of that representative group of our target customers that **rue21** should sell swimwear. We tested it, then rolled it out to our stores, and swimwear became a very significant part of our overall business. No data necessary. Just the insights of our **Customers**.

Another version of data science I practiced was to closely observe what other retailers were doing. The competitive data I studied told me that their profit margins for fragrance and beauty were 60 percent. That's all the data science I needed to see.

We built fragrance into a $50 million category, and beauty quickly ramped up to $15 million.

DON'T DROWN IN DATA

The exponential increase in data at our fingertips is mind-boggling. That presents its own challenges. The sheer volume and detail of data we can dive into easily can lull us into thinking all the number crunching has been done for us, and we have the answers we need. In general, the downside of the evolving metaverse—immersing us deeper and deeper into the digital ecosystem—is that it induces a certain laziness in how we think, act, react.

As technology advances, more rapidly by the day, each of us needs to prove our uniqueness and worth over and over again. Today's retailing business is so enamored with data it has lost sight of how much the intuition and *Feel* of its people have contributed to its sales successes over the years. It always has been a people business. It needs to balance cookie-cutter solutions from a spreadsheet with the imagination, spontaneity, and excitement that only people can provide.

That's *Back to the Future*.

If I can make any difference at all at *FIT*, I want it to be inspiring the students who go on to positions of influence to always put people as the number one priority and build around their talents to form a championship team.

That leads us to the big controversy of the Pandemic Age: *WFH* (*Work from Home*) or *WFO* (*Work from Office*) or *RTO* (*Return to Office*)?

I appreciate the pros and cons of both **WFH** and **WFO**. I urge you to make sure all sides of the situation are closely examined and evaluated honestly. I can accept that not everybody is returning to the office. That's just the new reality: the office culture has irrevocably changed.

Depending on your profession and where your career is at, it might make sense to work out of a living space, and it can work out well.

For others, though, I see an analogy between the overreliance on data in many areas of modern business management and an overreliance on **WFH**. Both represent the path of least resistance.

You know where that **Roadmap** leads you? Not to **Rule the World** but to the least desirable destination. Hiding out in a bedroom/home office is going through the motions instead of setting your bold, proprietary ideas in motion. People who get what they want fight for it. They don't effortlessly glide into it without struggling to some degree.

> **People who get what they want fight for it. They don't effortlessly glide into it without struggling to some degree.**

One of my favorite activities as a CEO or as a **Millennial Baby Boomer** (who is into **Mutual Mentoring**) always has been to interact with people—in person. My job was to **Motivate** them. I firmly believe **rue21** would not have been as successful if I had to manage people by Zoom.

Nevertheless, just like **This Book Is Not for the Timid**, it's also not for someone in the early stages of their career who mistakenly thinks **WFH** is equivalent to **WFO**. In no way is that a logical conclusion to reach. Why would you want to *avoid* the structured workplace instead of making yourself an **Integral** part of it?

WILL WFH HOLD YOU BACK?

Can a WFH worker adjust adequately to a new workplace's culture, policies, politics, work ethic, bosses, and coworkers, all without stepping foot in the office?

Whenever I'm with **Millennials** or **Gen Zers** who voice disapproval or stress about the thought of having to go to an office three or four days a week, I'm at a loss for words. (Not really. That rarely, if ever, happens.) My question to them is, "What is your definition of **Fulfillment**?"

Is it challenging yourself and meeting or exceeding the challenge? Can you effectively compete for a promotion with peers who are in the office if you are not?

To reflexively let go of proven practices and discount the value we place on human capital dishonors our **Past**.

Whether it's feeling a garment or working in an office, by holding on to the most valuable experiences and practices of our **Past**, we enrich our **Future**.

That's **Back to the Future**.

So what are you **Learning** from the **Past** to protect your **Future**?

RULES OF REINVENTION

GET A FEEL

Here are helpful notes for the *Humanology 101* lesson plan that I live by every day:

- *Weaponize Listening* (and *Speaking*) — Use the *Knowledge* you acquire through focused *Listening* to impress on the people you work with and for that you are constantly *Focused*. When you speak, make sure you are *Listenable* by not rambling or by always bringing a conversation back to you. Speak *Plainly* and *Directly*. Don't play verbal games with people if you want to be *Trusted* and *Respected*.

- *Care about People* — How do you show *Empathy* to others? By asking questions about them and their family. By offering help if they are in a bad way. Don't forget about—and don't be afraid of—trusting your *Feel*.

- *Mirror, Mirror on the Wall* — If you experience negative reactions to you, try to see yourself as others see you. At the end of each day, review your actions and grade yourself.

- *Don't Be a Prima Donna* — If your boss wants to contact you off-hours, like the weekend, so what? Consider it a privilege they need to ask you or tell you something. Prize that Saturday night call from the boss as if it is gold. In its own way, it is.

- *Show Confidence* — In yourself, of course. But also in those you work with and depend on. If there's a reason not to have Confidence in others on whom you depend, refer back to Care about People—find out what the problem is and try to help because if they are part of your own family or your professional family, by doing that, you'll also be helping yourself. You're only as good as the people around you. Don't get down on yourself. Instead of having an anxiety attack, attack life as the adventure it is. Every day.

THE *NEW* ROARING '20S

IN EARLY 2021 I looked at the state of our country and of the world and felt in my bones that we were headed for a ***New Roaring '20s***.

I didn't think it would start right away. Far from it. We still were paralyzed by the pandemic, both physically and mentally. I was looking further ahead to when COVID-19 and its variants would be, if not totally eliminated, at least under control, thanks to vaccinations, herd immunity, and sensible caution.

Then we all would be ready to break out from a very long social slumber to start enjoying life more fully once again.

To bring back the glamour and the excitement that marked one of America's most colorful eras isn't going to happen on its own, though. It's going to take extraordinary and selfless effort by each of us to make it happen and to make it last.

Are you ready to rock the ***New Roaring '20s***?

I am!

If you wonder why the years 1920–1929 are romanticized in our cultural history as one big playful, perpetual party, it's because people felt they were long overdue for enjoying life to the fullest. Who can blame them? They had just suffered through a prolonged period of devastating death and disease.

That famous era of nonstop energy, excitement, and entertainment followed the 1918 Spanish flu, just as ours is following the COVID-19 pandemic. If you think our situation these past few years has been oppressive, be thankful you weren't around one hundred years ago.

FIRE AND ICE

I bring that up not to be morbid but because it is the best way to explain the mindset of the 1920s public, which we easily can relate to currently: First, it's living in daily fear of death during the height of the pandemic (a modern-day plague). Second, it's experiencing the unleashed elation following the pandemic when people were itching to burst out and celebrate simply still being alive by enjoying life to the fullest as fast and frequently as possible.

A century ago America had just emerged the victor in World War I (1914–1918) at a cost of 100,000 deaths. That's a terrible toll, but it's one-tenth the size of the unthinkable body count that piled up during eighteen months of a deadly, contagious pandemic that occurred in 1918–1919. Imagine if 3 million people had died from COVID-19. That's how bad it was during the so-called Spanish flu, when the country's population was only 120 million, and the pandemic took 1 million lives.

The mortality rate then was unimaginably worse than for COVID-19 and its variants. Where the elderly were the most vulnerable to succumbing to COVID-19, the century-old pandemic known as the Spanish flu affected the youngest members of society to a horrible degree.

Children not yet five years old were particularly susceptible. According to **John M. Barry**'s book *The Great Influenza*, within a ten-week period youngsters in that age range died at a rate equal today to the frequency of deaths for all causes *for a period of twenty-three years*.

THE FATAL FLU

Not that older people were safe from the Spanish flu either. Barry also points to a study by insurance giant that reported "3.6 percent of all industrial workers ages twenty-five to forty-five died within the period of a few weeks." The fatal flu was so pervasive it is said to have shortened life expectancy by ten years.

It's no wonder that, after fighting their way back from prolonged battles that gravely threatened the country's well-being, Americans were ready to let loose. *And let loose they did!*

Think of the ecstatic, full-throated roar of a stadium full of sports fans whose team has just won a world championship, then magnify it millions of times to equal the roar of an entire country, cheering and celebrating its own recovery. That's how huge a roar the 1920s made.

People kicked up their heels on the dance floor doing the Charleston. New trends in fashion became all the rage. The optimism from coast to coast was flaunted by people wearing fancy clothes and stuffing their closets with a different outfit for every occasion.

Ladies loved bell hats, beaded dresses, feather headbands, and long pearl necklaces. Men looked sharp in three-piece suits, patent leather shoes, raccoon coats, leather jackets, and many styles of hats, from fedora and homburg to the ultraformal top hat.

Especially in the aftermath of being away from the office and dressed down while working from home, for the *New Roaring '20s*, I see a similar surge in the urge to dress up and go out on the town. As office workers return, so will after-hours meet-ups and the club scene. Chilly social distancing will warm up from body heat generated by close-up social contact.

Makeup will be bigger than before too, now that we want our faces to shine again after being unmasked.

People want to feel good about themselves. Don't you?

BOOTLEG BOOZE BUZZ

Americans in the rollicking *Roaring '20s* were drinking it all in, literally. The federal prohibition of alcohol created the irresistible mystique of speakeasies and backfired on the government, making the "forbidden fruit" of liquor more desirable and more intoxicating than it had been when legal. True to human nature, the sensation

THE OLD ROARING '20s

of doing something illicit gave those indulging in bootleg booze a bonus buzz.

The *New Roaring '20s* will experience a different form of intoxication. Alcohol's been legal for nearly a century now, but there's a new buzz being born for this *Roaring '20s* that lights up social gatherings: the end of prohibition—cannabis prohibition, that is—in states that have legalized sales and smoking lounges to accommodate marijuana users.

Where there once were speakeasies in the first *Roaring '20s* (to circumvent the federal prohibition of alcohol sales and consumption), there now in selected states (where it is legalized) are cannabis sales and lounges.

The illicit nature of drinking a banned substance during prohibition added to its sexy nature. Cannabis is a different type of party favor than alcohol, though. Depending on the strength and effect of a particular blend, enjoying it may lead to low-key chilling rather than dancing the night away, which is one of the most iconic images associated with the euphoric atmosphere of the first *Roaring '20s*.

It was a time of great awakening, sparked by a titillating new sensation of liberation. Young women who pushed back against the outmoded, unwritten rules of society were called "flappers."

THE NEW ROARING '20s

LIVE AND LET LIVE

Their open defiance was punctuated by happily chopping off their long hair—a radical move at the time—and by smoking cigarettes, another poke in the eye of the uptight establishment. The flappers' statement was loud and clear: "I can live my life as I like, with or without your approval."

As spiritual descendants of those *Roaring '20s*, we know something ourselves about dealing with national trauma. Now we owe it to ourselves to bounce back from adversity with the same optimism and energy that electrified the 1920s.

Our job is to pick ourselves up, wipe off the rust, and get back to work rebuilding our economy, our culture, and our social life. In the process, we'll be able to rip a page from history to create an updated version of those heady days—the *New Roaring '20s*!

I've always had good instincts about where things are going, but I don't claim to be an expert. Someone who can claim to be just that, though, is *Nicholas Christakis*. He is a sociologist and doctor who teaches at *Yale University*, where he also runs the Human Nature Lab.

He wrote a book, released in October 2020, called *Apollo's Arrow*, which looks at "The Profound and Enduring Impact of Coronavirus on the Way We Live."

As we progress toward the middle years of the 2020s, says Dr. Christakis, "I think that's going to feel a little like the *Roaring '20s* in the last century. People will relentlessly seek out social opportunities after being cooped up for so long. They'll flock to nightclubs, bars, restaurants, sporting events, concerts, and parties. We might see a rise in sexual licentiousness. And I expect the economy to boom and the arts to flourish as our tendency to socialize goes into overdrive."

Hard not to get very excited about how that sounds, right, especially coming from a highly respected scholar who studies how people behave for a living?

I see it mostly the same way.

A WORLD OF CHANGE

But I also have my own way of looking at the onset of another *Roaring '20s*. It's important to look deeper into things to discover less obvious outcomes so we can prepare ourselves to deal with them successfully.

We should not be surprised by constantly changing circumstances. We should take control of them too so we can take advantage of them. We should not only think about how a changing world will affect us but also how we can influence and help each other in a meaningful way that has an effect on the world around us.

I remind everyone that no matter what changes we've lived through with the pandemic, don't assume trends that have emerged recently will stay that way. A lot of people are convinced hybrid work (splitting up working from home and from an office) is here to stay. But no one knows for sure. Everybody's guessing, so the smart play is to keep your mind open, along with your options.

Dr. Christakis describes the bullish general atmosphere that will take hold in our culture as the pandemic recedes, the public health improves, and the economy revs up again. Advanced technologies already are creating

> We should not only think about how a changing world will affect us but also how we can influence and help each other in a meaningful way that has an effect on the world around us.

new career opportunities as well as making our work more efficient and expanding time for personal pleasures.

One hundred years ago saw the popularization of automobiles, radio, television—and even air travel began to take flight in a meaningful way.

A NEW, IMMERSIVE REALITY

Today we have the advent of a *Roaring '20s* with electric, self-driving vehicles and where AI and the metaverse hold in store immersive experiences that promise to create new forms of reality—or to challenge what we think of as reality.

Let's not forget, though, with all these reasons for optimism, that there's a dark side to all of this—as there is whenever the future rushes up to meet us while we're still adjusting to its newness. How do we prepare for it? How do we treat it responsibly so we don't turn into androids controlled by AI?

My answer to that is we need to embrace the benefits of inter-generational bonding practices, such as *Mutual Mentoring* and, significantly, *Mental Mentoring*.

Dr. Christakis makes timely comments on the critical ways people need people: "We befriend and love each other, we cooperate with each other, we teach and learn from each other."

It's that last part—teach and learn—that I see as our individual roles in creating and enjoying the new *Roaring '20s*. But it's more than a role that we play. It's not an act. It's a responsibility.

The 1920s certainly were not all fun and games. What's too easily overlooked about the old *Roaring '20s* is the antisocial sentiment that poisoned the air. During the 1920s Native Americans were being marginalized and persecuted, while immigrants of all ethnicities were stereotyped and demonized.

Some things don't change, even after one hundred years. We're seeing it again today in the stormy state of race relations, with social unrest reminding us how far we still have to go in denouncing intolerance and reversing ignorance.

PROGRESS THROUGH DISRUPTION

We can do better. America is a rapidly evolving, multicultural, and multicolored *melting pot*. Before racial justice can become a natural reflex in society, we need to forge race relations that are mutually **Respectful**, **Tolerant**, and marked by open minds who **Listen** and **Empathize**.

In my business life, I've always been known as a **Disruptor**, and I am proud of it. Why? Because **Disruption** and rejection of an outdated and unproductive status quo—kept in place for the wrong reasons—is called **Progress**.

Much of the "roar" of the twentieth century's '20s came from the younger generations of the time. Their hormones fueled the nation's pent-up energy, and their modern outlook encouraged freedom of expression and creativity.

That's the role today's younger generations are poised to play for the **New Roaring '20s**. As someone who **Mentors** them, and advocates **Mutual Mentoring** between generations, I'm rarin' to roar along with them and to help them navigate what could be rough waters in the wake of very stressful and unusual work conditions and living conditions.

That's why my advocacy of **Mutual Mentoring** is more important than ever. In a world where home offices and hybrid workplaces are trending, you can't just easily pop into someone's office down the hallway to seek help with a problem that might be work-related or might be personal. Not having someone accessible to confide in and seek solace from can be dangerously unhealthy.

The new way of working brings with it new mental wellness issues to consider. Connectedness to another human being—not just a screen or other digital device—is more important than ever to manage the pandemic of mental health issues through **Mental Mentoring**.

No matter what generation we belong to, there's enough anxiety to go around, so we need to watch out for each other more than ever. That's the first order of business. It's **Millennials** helping out **Gen Z**, just as **Baby Boomers** like me **Mentor Millennials**. After all, **Gen Z** and **Millennials** are next in line to take over the world. We need to help them on their way, not get in their way.

Working in a centralized office affects more than your job. It influences your social connections too.

AFTER-HOURS DILEMMA

That raises the question of how a worker's choice of location (home office or company office) can affect their social life. Hanging out with coworkers after-hours at a local watering hole or fitness class is a logical way to decompress while still being able to talk shop in an informal environment and, if so inclined, to meet someone.

With a home office as the base of operations, and with a pandemic shift to younger workers moving back in with their parents, how does isolation from coworkers create a confident social persona? At the end of the day, you log out of your workstation and leave your living space to ... go where? And meet who?

Does being apart from a central business district—where you are at home, virtually interconnected to coworkers during the day but physically disconnected at night—risk a new kind of loneliness?

The disconnect from a regular rhythm of interpersonal contact is bound to have a lasting impact on society and its inhabitants. It can't help but take a mental health toll that we all must acknowledge and work to overcome. We can fight it by being more creative and positive than ever.

Some optimism can be found in the knowledge that corporate America is investing more in mental health resources for their workers. Of course the flip side of that good news is that our healthcare system will be stretched to capacity and beyond.

MENTAL HEALTHCARE

Also encouraging is the new technology that has emerged more prominently during the pandemic. Such resources as therapy apps and telemedicine. Such advances give people more immediate access to mental health support that is faster and broader. They are not a replacement for visiting a doctor's office but an alternative or supplement, especially if the patient's need is urgent. Bullish venture capitalists have invested more than $2 billion in the growth industry of digital tools for personal health.

The *New Roaring '20s* is prime time for you to roar your individuality. It's not only about roaring in the social media sense, though. Social media can be an effective marketing tool when used smartly by experienced and savvy social media managers. It also can be used to have fun, as a relaxing form of amusement to connect with others and share sentiments about common interests.

But beware, social media also can be a major time suck that doesn't produce useful outcomes. If it's a marketing tool for your brand, why waste time (and maybe money) chasing after followers who aren't even part of your target audience?

If the appeal of social media for you is to mainly draw attention to yourself and socialize, have fun with it, make new friends with it, but don't let it grow out of proportion to your primary purpose—a *Purposeful, Fulfilling Life*.

When it's misused, social media can cause more problems than it's worth. It's like a fun house mirror that distorts reality. It induces emotional distress. Don't mistake it as a satisfying substitute for human connectedness. And if the nasty nature of some social media—shaming, trolling, bullying, FOMO—gets in your way, get it out of the way. Don't let yourself be a victim of social media's dark side.

The tough part about what we're going through in postpandemic society, which is destined to leave its mark on future generations, is that nobody knows anything about its aftereffects. We can think how we work and where we work has changed forever. That doesn't mean it has, though. It can revert back to what it was ever so slowly that we barely notice it is happening.

NOTHING IS FOREVER

Don't give up hope if you think your current situation is beyond repair for some reason. Think of the *New Roaring '20s* as a time of change—personal change. If you don't accept or feel comfortable with what is happening in the world around you, work harder to protect yourself from being adversely affected by it. Nothing in this world—or in this life—is guaranteed. What you know to be true today can be turned on its head tomorrow.

If you're flying high now, don't ignore the potential for things to sour quickly and find ways to minimize your risk.

If you're struggling now, don't give up hope that things can get better. You need to double down on turning your fortunes around.

What do you think the economy will be like in the next two years? What are you doing to prepare for any eventuality, whether economic boom or downturn? You do have some control over how external forces will affect you.

The key to insuring yourself against tough times is to stay informed, stay alert, and stay the course. That will go a long way toward your not overreacting or underreacting while staying active to protect your own interests.

Now is the time for you to put your career into overdrive. Or maybe to reconsider your career if you're not satisfied with where you're going. I bet a lot of you reading this have an entrepreneurial idea for starting a new company right now. At least I hope so. We need that, and you're the ones who will help fuel the rebound, and rebuilding, of America.

Plan an excursion with friends—make your own *Roaring '20s* vacation. Make a pledge to yourself to put the pandemic behind and use it as motivation to pursue bold new goals. It's a gift to yourself as a reward for emerging from the pandemic with a more positive, fearless attitude.

If you don't accept or feel comfortable with what is happening in the world around you, work harder to protect yourself from being adversely affected by it.

SPIRIT OF UNITY

If you find yourself slumping into a funk—caused by anxiety, depression, apathy—don't hesitate to reach out to a family member or a peer or anyone you trust and respect and who you know has **Empathy** for others. Remember, that's one of my key words of **Get a Life**. Is it yours?

Put aside for a moment the thought and desire for material possessions. Let the **New Roaring '20s** be about the spirit of unity that comes from practicing **Integrity**, **Compassion**, and **Authenticity** with our fellow human beings.

No matter how different we may be in smaller ways—age, ethnicity, geography, upbringing—what's more important is that we are relatable to each other by having in common our humanity and the **Perseverance** that was required to make it through the pandemic.

Taking advantage of that **Connectedness**, we all can work together to create a soulful **New Roaring '20s** that is about **Renewal** and **Mutual Respect**.

If those who endured the original **Roaring '20s** could rebuild their individual lives and repair the social fabric one hundred years ago after surviving a much worse pandemic, we owe it to them and to all generations from here on to show the same **Grit** and **Resourcefulness**. It is all about learning from the past to move ahead in the right direction. It's a social responsibility we all have. One thing the **New Roaring '20s** can be known for is the **Roar** you feel inside by **Giving Back**.

What better time than the present to get **Back to the Future!**

RULES OF REINVENTION

DON'T SNORE. BE READY TO ROAR!

The new **Roaring '20s** is about celebrating the joy of giving back by helping others celebrate their **Individuality** and **Independence**. Here are some noteworthy tips on how to make your roar heard:

- Ask others how they're doing and if there's anything you can **Help** with.

- Be **Considerate** of others, especially in public places.

- Respect differences of **Ethnicity**, **Gender Identity**, **Beliefs**, and **Culture**.

- Hold yourself and others **Accountable** for actions.

- Stay **Motivated** and **Motivate** others.

- Think **Freely** and **Boldly**.

- Stay **Flexible** and **Adaptable**. The only limits are the ones you set.

- There is no age limit on **Reinventing** yourself.

- When others doubt you, double down on your will to **Succeed**.

- Don't let social media define who **You** are.

- **Learn** from the **Past** and make the most of the **Future**.

GET A LEGACY

AT THE END of hosting *The Tonight Show* for seventeen years, in 2009, host *Jay Leno* wanted to make a strong and unique statement about his *Legacy*. As funny as he was, Leno's "stunt" in this case was not at all about comedy. In fact, it was quite dramatic.

What Leno did that night in signing off has stuck with me ever since.

He brought on stage sixty-four people. None of them ever had worked on the show. None of them ever had appeared on the show. Ranging in age from infants to teenagers, all sixty-four had been born to members of the show's staff during the previous seventeen years!

Jay Leno then said, "That's what I'd like my *Legacy* to be. When these kids grow up and they go, 'Hey, Mom and Dad, where did you guys meet?' they're going to say they met on the stage of *The Tonight Show*."

That's what a *Legacy* is all about.

I ran specialty apparel retail chain *rue21* for fifteen-plus years. Jay Leno's compelling way of illustrating his **Legacy** got me to thinking about my own **Legacy**, not only at *rue21* but also beyond.

Why is that so important to me? The same reason it should be important to you. You work hard your whole life, and you'd like people to remember you a certain way long after you're no longer here in the flesh. That's human nature. We all have egos, so it's normal that we spend time thinking about our **Legacy**.

Jeff Erdmann, whom you met earlier in **Get a Life**, told me he has become more philanthropic through the years. "I love creating and helping nonprofits," he said. His pet projects include a soup kitchen in New York City and a summer program involving people from Iran called Lost Boys. When he sees what they accomplished, he hugs them and cries. There is nothing in his very successful business life that Jeff is prouder of than his giving back to the less privileged.

He has far-reaching reasons for his charitable work that go beyond his own gratification. "The biggest void in this country is leadership," said Jeff. With that in mind, he also endows scholarships at an all-boys school "to help create future leaders."

Like Jay Leno and Jeff Erdmann, I care **Passionately** about my **Legacy**.

I can't say it's foremost in my mind with every decision I make or every project I undertake. But even if it's not top-of-mind 24/7, it definitely plays a role in everything I do, even if subconsciously. Do you feel the same?

As much as I value how vital it is to nurture our **Legacies**, I wasn't fully prepared for the out-of-body experience of watching my **FIT Legacy**, through the award and **Mentorship** program I created, reach a climax in its first year of existence.

At the end of the *FIT* school year, a gala evening event is held where I present the $25,000 *Bob Fisch Entrepreneurial Award*.

The recipients are selected after a very thorough process. Tapping into my decades of *Tribal Knowledge* about how the world works, I leave no stone unturned in challenging the students to identify which of their ideas have the best chance of *Succeeding*.

For the first annual presentation in May 2022, I decided to double the stakes by awarding two checks of $25,000 each. (There actually were three recipients, with one of the checks presented to a team of two students working together on the same project.) Earlier in the year, I gave ten students scholarships of $5,500 each—five in Fashion Design and five in Global Fashion Management. In addition, I gave $1,000 to each of the second-year graduate students for their Capstone projects. *(For updates on FIT award recipients, go to MillennialBabyBoomer.com.)*

I especially appreciated *FIT* President Dr. Brown remarking, "How many graduate students can say a guardian angel came and touched them on the shoulder and said, 'Here, maybe you need this'? You are an extraordinary friend and benefactor for this group." She then went off script for a moment to kiddingly tell the students "Don't expect it ever to happen again, okay?"

I set up this program to *keep Paying It Forward* so that I can make it happen again and again to future *FIT* students. It's anything but a one-and-done deal I put together with *FIT*. It's my *Legacy*, and it means the world to me, just as *your Legacy* should mean the world to you, right?

Even more important than the money awarded is the extensive in-person *Mentoring* from me and *FIT* professors, who I work with closely to present an integrated and valuable *Mentoring* resource.

FIT professors do an excellent job teaching their students what I continually focus on with whomever I am *Mentoring*—think like the customer! The customer may not always be right, but they are the customer, so they need to be treated right.

The faculty's *Mentorship* skills are critical in shaping the future not only of their students' careers but also their personal lives. My job is to challenge the students, show them how to take their *Visions* to fruition, and generally do whatever I can to help their careers take flight.

THE JOY OF GIVING BACK

I take my role very seriously. It's well worth the considerable time and energy I devote to it. The gratification it brings surpasses anything I imagined when I left the corporate world to devote my life to *Mentoring* and *Giving Back*. I see it as a *Responsibility* we all eventually need to embrace.

There's a very strong bond that I felt with the *FIT* students, so much so that I joked at the awards ceremony that I never had someone at *rue21* quit on me after one year. Was I feeling a separation anxiety with the students who were about to graduate? You bet I did!

"You have really made a difference in my life because I love giving back, and with you I love giving back even more," I told them. "So I thank you for everything you have done for me." I couldn't have been more sincere in telling them that. It's a totally different feeling than I've ever had getting to know them. I was compelled to constantly send notes to them about how excited I was for them, and they'd send notes back to me.

One of the $25,000 award recipients, through tears, held on to the jumbo "photo prop" check as she said, "This really touched my heart because it means I can work with my friends and favorite human beings and really start the next phase of my career. So this really means a lot to me. My parents are in town from Korea, so I want to bring them the check."

Her emotional reaction and gratitude epitomize the meaning of *Legacy*—how we live our life inevitably touches other people in one way or another. It takes all of the human qualities discussed in this book to make sure your *Legacy* helps people. While it's nice to have the means to reward people financially, money is not a requirement of *Legacy*; it's icing on the cake.

HOW WILL YOU BE REMEMBERED?

The way to identify what you want your *Legacy* to be is to ask yourself "What is it I am working toward to achieve?" An *Authentic Legacy* is something you do that touches people deeply and permanently. If you are not already *Giving Back* to others, based on your accumulated wisdom and experience, how do you plan to *Give Back* in the future? Everybody's *Legacy* deserved serious thought. How do you want to be remembered?

A rich *Legacy* is one where you touch others with your contribution to their *Success* and *Self-Esteem*. Your influence doesn't end when you do. It goes on as a cherished part of their life for as long as they live.

When I left *rue21*, it was a particular point of pride that my *Legacy*

> A rich *Legacy* is one where you touch others with your contribution to their *Success* and *Self-Esteem*.

was as someone who was tough when necessary but fair, so people trusted me.

There is a lot that goes into legitimizing your *Legacy*. *Authenticity*, for one. You can't create a *Legacy*, for example, by doing your job on autopilot. You can create it, though, by digging deep to elevate your performance and that of everyone else who depends on you. You also can create it by caring about other people and hoping for their *Success* and helping them achieve it.

There's no such thing as having too much *Empathy* for others, but is there such a thing as having too much *Apathy*—not caring about others or even about your own future?

What I want to talk about here, though, is not just thinking about your *Legacy*. It's doing something about it! It doesn't just happen magically or overnight. It can take a lifetime.

It's not only people who have *Legacies*. So do eras in history. The *Legacy* of a particular period can be defined by war (Vietnam), or economic conditions (the Great Depression), or a cultural revolution (Woodstock Nation), or a public health crisis (COVID-19).

A CLASS BY ITSELF

Every generation can expect to experience at least one devastating event of historic proportion. But the COVID-19 pandemic is in a class by itself. I've never seen anything like it. Hardly anybody alive has. No matter what generation you belong to, we need to *Watch Out for Each Other* more than ever. That's the first order of business.

Whether or not we know someone who has been lost to it, the pandemic has affected each of us in ways other historic events have not. The ramifications of what the pandemic has done to our state of mind will shadow some people for a very long time.

The point is that when you're living through a historical *Legacy* that's evolving over time (like the pandemic), you need to assess how it will affect you and how you will respond to it. Do you give in to its pressures and challenges, or do you use them to motivate you, to forge a personal *Legacy* that withstands, and maybe even benefits from, the historical *Legacy*?

During the *Legacy* of COVID-19, how we manage our own *Legacies* has been tested as never before.

For instance, what will high school students in the class of 2021 see their *Legacy* as being when they look back a decade or more in the future?

Their unique—and traumatic—experience of being, in effect, "homeschooled" is something none of us ever had to cope with in our final year of high school. Instead of being school-bound every day, they were homebound almost every day.

In a graduation speech I came across, a high school senior told fellow students, "The shortcomings of your past should not define your future." Great advice! In fact, it's not a stretch to call the pandemic a shortcoming in all our lives. But it's not going to define my future! What about yours?

LEARNING TO BE BETTER

Can we learn from the past? Yes! We can learn from our past mistakes as well as our past successes. What's most important to our *Legacies* is that we learn how to make the present better and the future even better than that.

Only time will tell if living through the pandemic as a high school senior toughened them up or if "going to class" without leaving their bedroom gave them a false sense of comfort.

The same question can (and should) be asked of **Millennials** as well as **Gen Z** and, yes, even **Gen X**. Did the pandemic toughen them up? What about you? Did it change your personal outlook about what you're doing with your life? It should have!

If you believe adversity builds character and **Legacies**, the pandemic has given us a life's worth of **Motivation** to work with. The abrupt changes in how and where we work that were made necessary during the pandemic also point to some exciting opportunities for building **Legacies** as we move past the pandemic.

If there are silver linings coming out of COVID-19—and I strongly believe there are—one of them is that it has given people the freedom to rethink their career choices and their future. And their **Legacy**.

We beat the pandemic! A celebration is in order. It's an ideal time to move on. New thoughts and ideas and possibilities should surround you now. What better time to be **Fearless** and build a **Legacy** than in the midst of these liberating moments of exhilaration.

One of the commencement remarks that spoke to me was attributed to Navy SEAL and motivational author **David Goggins**, who said, "Life is one big tug-of-war between mediocrity and trying to find your best self."

AVOID MEDIOCRITY

Don't discount the possibility that working from home might lead to mediocrity in your performance, while being in the thick of the office action is the better place to discover your best self. While it's not true for everybody, depending on their individual circumstances, it's worth taking into account.

Step out of your **Comfort Zone**. Try things that may intimidate you.

I've always been a big believer that forming a positive *Legacy* has a lot to do with being *Authentic* and having *Loyalty* and *Trust*, the same way Jay Leno and his staff had mutual respect for one another. Would that have happened if they were working remotely?

The anthem for these times has become *We're All in This Together*. That's only half of it, though. The other half, regardless of generation, is "We all need to come out of this together, stronger and more united than before."

That's what life was like for me and hundreds of others at *rue21*. What a great feeling it was for me to go to work there knowing that people understood what they needed to do, knowing we could finish each other's sentences, and knowing we all could just spring into action to get the job done to everyone's satisfaction and beyond. That's because we formed a tight, smooth-running machine built on *Trust* and *Loyalty*. Would that have happened the same way if we were working remotely?

The challenge in building a worthwhile *Legacy* in these times is maintaining your morale. There are ways to combat the lengthy social disorder we've gone through, though. Use your *Ingenuity*—and your love of job security—to sustain your *Work Ethic* and your *Enthusiasm*. There's always something to do that can advance your career *Progress*. Whatever your choice, keep your mind *Focused*, *Fertile*, and *Agile*.

FAMILY AT WORK

We all need to get back to *Loyalty* and *Trust*. Like Leno, I am proud that the associates at *rue21* enjoyed working there and trust working there and enjoyed coming to work. Also like Leno, I, too, saw families forming and growing up during my fifteen years at *rue21*.

Do businesses need to re-instill in their employees that kind of camaraderie? Without question. But they can't do it without the willingness of employees. That comes down to the question of what will your pandemic *Legacy* be ten or twenty years from now.

Did you take full advantage of the sudden WFH culture to hide or to work even harder than you might have if you still were in the office? Did you use it to find or create better *Opportunities* for yourself? Maybe even start a side hustle that paid off? Times of adversity are when you can really establish your *Legacy*.

An entrepreneur starting a business that succeeds can be a wonderful *Legacy*. *Facebook* founder *Mark Zuckerberg* may not exactly be your typical example, but he is a high-profile example nonetheless.

At the same time, Zuckerberg has been criticized and questioned about his ethics because some of Facebook's policies have permitted dangerously false information to spread like destructive wildfire throughout the world.

There are good reasons that *Authenticity* and *Integrity* are essential elements of *Legacy*: The financial fortunes of a person or a business can, like the stock market, go up and down. It can be the result of internal business conditions that you control, or it can be because of external conditions, such as the economy, which you contribute to but can't otherwise control.

WHAT REALLY MATTERS

The only thing to hold on to, as far as your *Legacy* goes, is to be true to yourself, to be *Authentic* to others, and to at all times act with utmost scruples. When you're on your deathbed, reflecting on whether a business opened or closed, is hardly what's important.

Whether you treated customers and partners and employees and others **Honestly** and **Respectfully** is what really matters as you take stock of how well your time here was spent.

When your time is up, you don't want shortcomings of your past to define who you were. Even in the prime of life, you don't want shortcomings of your past to define who you still can become. At all times, the right attitude to adopt is *The Best Is Yet to Come*.

A **Legacy** to be proud of doesn't come without a lot of hard, sustained effort. So let me ask you, What is your life's **Legacy** so far?

Or should I say what *are* your life's **Legacies**? I believe we can have more than one, especially if you're a **Millennial** or younger because you could be going strong until your one hundredth birthday, with **Legacies** to spare!

We keep on creating and recreating our **Legacies**. If a **Legacy** we want to build is not going well, we have the **Opportunity**, even the **Responsibility**, to correct it, update it, upgrade it. **Responsibility** to who? To your family, perhaps. To friends who care about you. But most of all, to yourself.

Legacies are available at any and every point in life, age be damned! I live by my own Golden Rule that it doesn't matter in which year you were born or to which generation you belong. What matters to me is who you are, what you do, how young you allow yourself to be. If someone asks how old I am, my answer is *Ageless*. That's what yours should be too.

> **A *Legacy* to be proud of doesn't come without a lot of hard, sustained effort.**

GROWING "YOLDER"

Young. Old. There's actually a shorthand term that combines the two: **Yold**. You're thinking right now that the equation here is Young + Old = Yold. Not quite. You don't get to be **Yold**, which is to say a youthful (or **Millennial**) **Baby Boomer**, by adding up the years.

No. You earn the right to grow **Yold** by *subtracting* the years. By *defying* the years! And I defy anyone to prove me wrong.

Speaking of **Yold**, my greatest business success occurred after I turned fifty. I saw one of my **Legacies** as becoming chairman of **rue21** after serving as CEO for twenty years. That particular **Legacy** didn't pan out, but I'm not complaining because I have others that I cherish more than I could imagine. I find myself in a better place than I thought I'd ever be.

In the category of Big Business Moments, there's my **Cotton Crisis Legacy**. When just about every other apparel retailer bumped up prices in 2011 to pass along their increased cost of goods during the cotton shortage, we held firm on our prices. My aggressively positive predictions on our sales performance for the holiday season shocked Wall Street analysts and investors to the point that we moved the market. I am very proud of that **Legacy**.

How I handled the **Cotton Crisis** is consistent with my preference for going against the grain, being a **Disruptor**, and thinking independent of so-called "conventional wisdom." That, too, is part of my **Legacy**.

DON'T CONFUSE ISSUES WITH LOGIC

As I mentioned earlier in this book, it's a mistake to confuse issues with logic. I always looked at the public as my customer, and I needed to take good care of them. If I was running a business during a period of inflation, with prices on the rise, I would not automatically jack up prices. I'm disappointed when decision-makers don't take a stand and stabilize prices. Instead, they fall back on predictably reactionary positions. That's not a *Legacy* I'd be proud to have.

Where I take great pride is in my *Legacy* of treating female employees no different from male employees. As one of the chapters in my previous book declares, "Bob's Club Is No Boys Club." If anything, there were men who worked for me who would say that *rue21* women were at an advantage over them. If they were, it's because those women earned that advantage. To me, gender is secondary to performance.

How I handled the *Cotton Crisis* and respected female employees as equal to male employees are like mini-*Legacies* within my overall *rue21 Legacy* of building a juggernaut retailer from the ground up.

In fact, it wouldn't be wrong to say I built it from *under* the ground up because when I got there, the company was just about to go under. Another *Legacy* within the *Legacy* is the forty-five consecutive quarters over eleven years of not once missing a sales and profit projection.

Now I am living my post-*rue21 Legacies*: becoming a published author at Forbes Books with *Fisch Tales* and serving as a *Mentor* and scholarship provider for graduate students in the fashion and merchandising programs at *FIT* as well as helping bolster the school's reputation because it deserves the recognition.

LOOKING FOR NEW LEGACIES

The publishing *Legacy* continues with this book, and I look forward to fulfilling another *Legacy* I have been thinking about for years—working in a *Mentoring* capacity with staff for the Miami Heat NBA franchise.

I am optimistic by nature, and that explains the bullishness of one of my predictions about a shared *Legacy* we are staring in the face: the advent of a *New Roaring '20s* that reprises the famous party-hearty decade of the twentieth century that sparks the imagination and continues to be the stuff of legend.

I absolutely believe that we are poised to ring in another *Roaring '20s*, with the difference that it ends unlike the original version.

By embracing the benefits of *Intergenerational Bonding* practices such as *Mutual Mentoring* and *Mental Mentoring*, let's make it happen.

Thanks to the internet and the proliferation of digital apps that support individualized business models, *the Sky's the Limit* to create your own *Legacy* out of your own *Passion*!

The most blunt advice I saw, which I totally agree with, comes from NYU professor *Scott Galloway*.

His advice for those in the early stages of building a career boils down to three things: 1) work your ass off to be great at something,

2) make small investments in relationships every day, and 3) invest in being physically fit.

Galloway adds, "This BS about work-life balance is BS." I agree with that too. If you're focusing on a *Legacy* that emphasizes work-life balance, to me, it says you're already thinking about how much time you want to spend *not* working.

However, if you focus simply on working your ass off, as Galloway says, the personal time you need will be one of the fruits of your labor. But you don't plan for it *before* the hard work is done. You earn it *after* the hard work is done.

My idea of the ideal *Legacy* is to help people grow and realize their dreams. A *Legacy* is not simply about slapping your name on a building. That's nice if you can afford it, but it's not the highest form of *Giving Back* no matter how much money changes hands.

Instead, the purest form of *Legacy* is fostering relationships with people to see them flourish when you're around—and continue to prosper when you're no longer around. The pleasure is seeing people (not unlike seeing your own children) develop and make something of themselves that makes you proud of them and of yourself. That's your *Legacy*.

So what are you waiting for?

Get out there and ***Get a Life***!

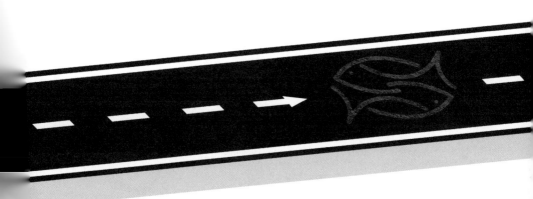

RULES OF REINVENTION

BOB FISCH'S TOP TEN LEGACY BUILDERS

A *Legacy* is not given to you. Unlike a *Calling*, it's *not* a gift from above. It's a monument to your life's work, and you're the only one who can build it, with your own hands, from the ground up. So get out there and *Get a Legacy* or forever regret letting yourself down (as well as disappointing those who believe in you). I'll get you started with *Bob Fisch's Top Ten Legacy Builders* below. Then you're off and running to *Rule the World*!

- *Be Kind* to others. Not only for your own sake but also because you want to be the *Kind* of person who compensates for the world's *unkind* people, of which there are way too many.

- *Respect* yourself. Live the highest-quality *Personal Values* described throughout this book. How can you expect to *Respect* others who deserve it unless you start with *number one*?

- Be *Fearless* in standing up for your *Beliefs*. One last time ... *This Book Is Not for the Timid*!

- Take *Risks* outside your *Comfort Zone*. If a nice 'n' easy, laid-back life is all you crave, that's where you'll end up—in *back* of the pack.

- Follow and feed your *Passion*. That's where your life's momentum and nourishment comes from. Without *Passion*, prepare to starve to death.

- Stay *Humble*. Don't pay attention to the blowhards who talk a lot more than they achieve. *Humility* displays *Strength of Character.*

- Don't *Overthink* things. Specifically, *Don't Confuse Issues with Logic*. There's a lot to be said for trusting your *Feel*.

- *Ask* questions. Life is a never-ending *Lesson*. Be a sponge around people who know valuable things that you don't.

- Don't give up *Individuality*. Acting like a sheep is baa-d news!

- Don't let the *Negativity* of others *Discourage* you. Tell them to *Get a Life*!

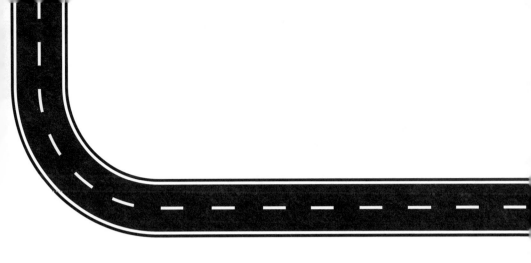

MEET THE MILLENNIAL ADVISORY BOARD

I CHOSE THESE INDIVIDUALS for their range of expertise and interests to advise me on this book and on future iterations of the *Millennial Baby Boomer* franchise. (The profiles are arranged in alphabetical order.)

At the end of this section, I encourage you to complete your own profile (no matter your age) using the blank form we've provided for you. I'm confident that you'll discover interesting aspects of your persona you haven't thought a lot about, and as a bonus, you will enjoy doing it.

The Best Is Yet to Come!

BRUCE APAR

GIGS I HAVE KNOWN
- Writer/Editor/Publisher
- Volunteer/Fundraiser
- Actor
- Punslinger
- Son/Brother/Husband/Father

LIVING PLACES I HAVE KNOWN
- Astoria (Queens, New York)
- Franklin Square (Long Island, New York)
- Syracuse (Upstate New York)
- Philadelphia (Pennsylvania)
- East Northport (Long Island, New York)
- Yorktown Heights (Westchester County, New York)

MENTOR(S) I HAVE KNOWN My superego

ONE WORD Resilient

ALTER EGO Actor

OBSESSION Words

NO-COMFORT ZONE
(What I have done or want to do outside my comfort zone)
- Stand-up comedy

WHAT THE MAB TEAM MEANS TO ME
- A clubhouse for sharing perspectives to gain mutual understanding through intergenerational bonding

NICOLE MANAFI CAMPBELL

GIGS I HAVE KNOWN
- Investment Banking Analyst
- VP of Business Development and Investor Relations
- Partnerships Lead at a digital health start-up

LIVING PLACES I HAVE KNOWN
- San Francisco Bay Area
- New York City

MENTOR(S) I HAVE KNOWN Bob Fisch, the bosses I've been lucky enough to have had in my career so far

ONE WORD Collaboration

ALTER EGO Anthony Bourdain (for having told stories and narratives in a way that made people gravitate toward learning about new cultures)

OBSESSION The way I feel whenever I see a Mercedes-Benz G-Wagon. I stop in my tracks and stare in awe and admiration whenever the car that people tend to either love or hate drives by

NO-COMFORT ZONE
(What I have done or want to do outside my comfort zone)
- Working and living abroad to challenge the status quo and provide lifelong learning opportunities

WHAT THE MAB TEAM MEANS TO ME
- Community, friendship, and discussions that spark joy and are led by diversity of thought and experience

JULIE FANNING

GIGS I HAVE KNOWN
- Managing boutiques
- Managing website content and assisting creative directors for children's fashion company
- General Manager at Equinox Flatiron (New York City)

LIVING PLACES I HAVE KNOWN
- New York City
- San Francisco

MENTOR(S) I HAVE KNOWN
- Matthew Plotkin, Wil Diaz, Lawrence Sanders, Brian Grogin (all Equinox)
- Ann Byington
- My family
- Bob Fisch, Millennial Baby Boomer®

ONE WORD Humorous

ALTER EGO Trinity (from The Matrix film series)

OBSESSION
- How can I be better today than I was yesterday
- Creating a safe, fun, successful space at work

NO-COMFORT ZONE
(What I have done or want to do outside my comfort zone)
- Joining the Millennial Advisory Board was a huge step; it has been an incredibly freeing experience to step outside my work and do something on my own.

WHAT THE MAB TEAM MEANS TO ME
- It allows me to use my voice, speak up, have an opinion. I've never felt like I had that in me and finally feel like I can make an impact.

BOB FISCH

GIGS I HAVE KNOWN

- *FIT* Advisor, Speaker, Mentor, Graduate School Awards Program sponsor
- *FIT* Foundation Board of Directors
- Forbes Books Author of *Fisch Tales: The Making of a Millennial Baby Boomer* and *Get a Life: Roadmap to Rule the World*
- *rue21* Founder and Former Chairman, CEO
- Board of Directors, Ollie's Bargain Outlet
- Advisor, Investor—XRC Labs

LIVING PLACES I HAVE KNOWN

- Miami heat
- NYC cool
- West Hartford burbs

MENTOR(S) I HAVE KNOWN Dr. Paul Vahanian, Tom Unrine

ONE WORD Feisty

ALTER EGO Restaurant influencer, rock star Adam Levine

OBSESSION

- Miami Heat
- Opportunity of another home—three is not enough!
- *Sneakers!* Lots of them!
- Pushing people to get outside their comfort zone and to take risks so they maximize their potential.

NO-COMFORT ZONE
(What I have done or want to do outside my comfort zone)

- Working for someone else ... NOT!
- Local driving in Miami

WHAT THE MAB TEAM MEANS TO ME

- Totally giving back, leading, and mentoring the MAB team to broaden their biz/life horizons and experiences

STEPHANIE FISCH

GIGS I HAVE KNOWN
- Developing best-selling fragrances at *rue21*
- Trendspotting
- Department Store Buyer

LIVING PLACES I HAVE KNOWN
- Miami Beach
- Manhattan
- Connecticut

MENTOR(S) I HAVE KNOWN
- Glo and Ron Pallot
- Bob Fisch
- Carole Schragis

ONE WORD Energy

ALTER EGO QVC host

OBSESSION
- Living my brand
- Family
- Inspiring those around me

NO-COMFORT ZONE
(What I have done or want to do outside my comfort zone)

- Spin instructor
- Traveling to Buton
- Fashion designer

WHAT THE MAB TEAM MEANS TO ME
- Group mentoring, fueling relationships and collaborative intergeneration connections, gaining new perspectives and unlocking new potentials

RICK HARTMANN

GIGS I HAVE KNOWN

- Global Property Facultative Underwriter, Gen Re
- Treaty Account Executive, Gen Re
- Senior Vice President – Treaty Broking, Guy Carpenter

LIVING PLACES I HAVE KNOWN

- Wallingford (Pennsylvania)
- Philadelphia
- Newtown (Pennsylvania)

MENTOR(S) I HAVE KNOWN
Mom (Christine Hartmann Orlando), Ms. D. C. Pixie Roane, Strath Haven, sixth-grade health and physical education, Mr. Mark Jankowksi, president, Amplified Learning, Mr. John Stone, Gen Re, Mr. Rick Ruggiero, Gen Re, Mr. Bob Fisch

ONE WORD
Tenacity

ALTER EGO
James Bond

OBSESSION

- Thinking differently and being different to never settle for pretty good
- Being a father my daughters can look up to
- To become a CEO

NO-COMFORT ZONE
(What I have done or want to do outside my comfort zone)

- Have presented to audiences with over three hundred attendees
- After ten years with a single employer, I changed career pathways
- Pursuing Executive MBA

WHAT THE MAB TEAM MEANS TO ME

- Accountability. Hard workers and authentic individuals who have achieved success in various fields. We are direct, and we keep pushing each other.

JEFFREY LITTMAN

GIGS I HAVE KNOWN
- Power Market Consultant > Advised utilities how to economically reach their carbon emission goals
- Energy Storage Analyst > Determine the most profitable places to build large-scale energy storage batteries

LIVING PLACES I HAVE KNOWN
- Miami Beach
- Washington, D.C.

MENTORS I HAVE KNOWN
- My family
- Bob Fisch
- Ben Stravinsky
- David Goggins

ONE WORD Focus

ALTER EGO Jason Sommerville (famous poker player and online streamer)

OBSESSION Health, Family, Sustainable energy, Music, Cooking, Fitness, Poker, Behavioral economics, E-sports

NO-COMFORT ZONE
- Running length of the South Beach Boardwalk (equivalent of about a half-marathon)
- Started a new job where I have partial expertise, hoping to enhance my career

WHAT THE MAB TEAM MEANS TO ME
- Perspective. Listening to people with different backgrounds from what I normally would encounter on a day-to-day basis offers a grounding effect.

DESIREE "DEZZ" NUNES

GIGS I HAVE KNOWN

- Investment Management Specialist on the Erdmann Team, Merrill Lynch Private Wealth Management
- Associate, Client, and Partner Group, Private Wealth Partners, KKR & Co. Inc.

LIVING PLACES I HAVE KNOWN New York City

MENTOR(S) I HAVE KNOWN

- The MBB himself, Bob Fisch! Always pushing me to be my best self, step outside my comfort zone, and think differently. Challenges me when I need it most!

ONE WORD Commitment

ALTER EGO Kim Kardashian

OBSESSION

- Being my best self and building my career in an exciting new chapter
- Early morning gym routine

NO-COMFORT ZONE
(What I have done or want to do outside my comfort zone)

- Leaving my job of nine years in an industry that I have been in since I graduated college for a new role at a new firm
- Taking my first solo trip (to Spain)

WHAT THE MAB TEAM MEANS TO ME

- An exciting group where I can participate in stimulating and thoughtful discussions, share interesting ideas and current events, and feel connections across different generations!

DIONE O'DELL

GIGS I HAVE KNOWN
- Vice President, Marketing, *rue21*
- Realtor/member of Beaver County Association of Realtors and NAR
- Owner, The Gardenia Branch boutique

LIVING PLACES I HAVE KNOWN
- My small piece of heaven tucked away in the Enon Valley (Pennsylvania) countryside

MENTOR(S) I HAVE KNOWN
- Bob Fisch
- Gaye Campbell
- My parents, whom I admire and adore

ONE WORD Balance

ALTER EGO *Solid Gold* dancer

OBSESSION Party planning

NO-COMFORT ZONE
(What I have done or want to do outside my comfort zone)
- Opening a new business during the COVID-19 pandemic

WHAT THE MAB TEAM MEANS TO ME
- A passionate group of smart and inspiring individuals who support, listen, encourage, share, and mentor each other to enable the evolution of goodness and success

BRIAN TUNICK

GIGS I HAVE KNOWN
- #1 Ranked Research Analyst at JPMorgan
- Cofounder of ESG Software Platform
- Founder of Family Office

LIVING PLACES I HAVE KNOWN
- New York City, Jacksonville Beach

MENTOR(S) I HAVE KNOWN
- Steve Kernkraut
- Dana Telsey
- Bob Fisch

ONE WORD Execution

ALTER EGO Roger Federer

OBSESSION
- Tennis
- Mentoring
- Seeing others succeed

NO-COMFORT ZONE
(What I have done or want to do outside my comfort zone)
- Cofounding a start-up and working in the nonprofit world

WHAT THE MAB TEAM MEANS TO ME
- As a mentor myself, I always come away with some fresh ideas.

YOUR PROFILE!

GIGS I HAVE KNOWN

LIVING PLACES I HAVE KNOWN

MENTOR(S) I HAVE KNOWN

ONE WORD

ALTER EGO

OBSESSION

NO-COMFORT ZONE
(What I have done or want to do outside my comfort zone)

WHAT *GET A LIFE* MEANS TO ME